The Sugar Witch

by

Nathan Sanders

New York Hollywood London Toronto

SAMUELFRENCH.COM

Copyright © 2008 by Nathan Sanders

Original cover illustration and typography © 2008 Andy Markley - Art101.com, with thanks to Dan Sparks

ALL RIGHTS RESERVED

CAUTION: Professionals and amateurs are hereby warned that *THE SUGAR WITCH* is subject to a royalty. It is fully protected under the copyright laws of the United States of America, the British Commonwealth, including Canada, and all other countries of the Copyright Union. All rights, including professional, amateur, motion picture, recitation, lecturing, public reading, radio broadcasting, television and the rights of translation into foreign languages are strictly reserved. In its present form the play is dedicated to the reading public only.

The amateur live stage performance rights to *THE SUGAR WITCH* are controlled exclusively by Samuel French, Inc., and royalty arrangements and licenses must be secured well in advance of presentation. PLEASE NOTE that amateur royalty fees are set upon application in accordance with your producing circumstances. When applying for a royalty quotation and license please give us the number of performances intended, dates of production, your seating capacity and admission fee. Royalties are payable one week before the opening performance of the play to Samuel French, Inc., at 45 W. 25th Street, New York, NY 10010.

Royalty of the required amount must be paid whether the play is presented for charity or gain and whether or not admission is charged.

Stock royalty quoted upon application to Samuel French, Inc.

For all other rights than those stipulated above, apply to: Mistral Artist Management, 609 Greenwich St. #4B, New York, 10014 Attn: Jerome Henry Rudes.

Particular emphasis is laid on the question of amateur or professional readings, permission and terms for which must be secured in writing from Samuel French, Inc.

Copying from this book in whole or in part is strictly forbidden by law, and the right of performance is not transferable.

Whenever the play is produced the following notice must appear on all programs, printing and advertising for the play: "Produced by special arrangement with Samuel French, Inc."

Due authorship credit must be given on all programs, printing and advertising for the play.

ISBN 978-0-573-66364-2

No one shall commit or authorize any act or omission by which the copyright of, or the right to copyright, this play may be impaired.

No one shall make any changes in this play for the purpose of production.

Publication of this play does not imply availability for performance. Both amateurs and professionals considering a production are strongly advised in their own interests to apply to Samuel French, Inc., for written permission before starting rehearsals, advertising, or booking a theatre.

No part of this book may be reproduced, stored in a retrieval system, or transmitted in any form, by any means, now known or yet to be invented, including mechanical, electronic, photocopying, recording, videotaping, or otherwise, without the prior written permission of the publisher.

IMPORTANT BILLING AND CREDIT REQUIREMENTS

All producers of *THE SUGAR WITCH must* give credit to the Author of the Play in all programs distributed in connection with performances of the Play, and in all instances in which the title of the Play appears for the purposes of advertising, publicizing or otherwise exploiting the Play and/or a production. The name of the Author *must* appear on a separate line on which no other name appears, immediately following the title and *must* appear in size of type not less than fifty percent of the size of the title type.

Licensees are solely responsible for obtaining formal written permission from copyright owners to use copyrighted music in the performance of this play and are strongly cautioned to do so. If no such permission is obtained by the licensee, then the licensee must use only original music that the licensee owns and controls. Licensees are solely responsible and liable for all music clearances and shall indemnify the copyright owners of the play and their licensing agent, Samuel French, Inc., against any costs, expenses, losses and liabilities arising from the use of music by licensees.

CHARACTERS

SISSER (late 30s): Southern, obese, and somewhat mad. A wheel-chair-bound lover of Little Debbie snack cakes. Capable of anything – even murder.

RUTH ANN MEEKS (late 30s): Southern, racist, and half-insane. A "church-goer," plain, not very pretty. Most likely the product of incest.

ANNABELLE (50s): African-American; Southern swamp mystic and conjure woman. Brews magical potions from sugar cane molasses. The last in a long-line of powerful "sugar witches."

MOSES BEAN (mid 20s): Southern, handsome and boyish. A mechanic at the local Texaco station. Innocent and virginal; a "gender-reversed Sleeping Beauty."

HANK HARTLEY (30s): Southern, handsome and strong. The play's "gentleman caller." Recently returned to Sugar Bean to take over his family's funeral home business. Madly "in-love" yet hiding a dark secret.

GRANDDADDY MEEKS (60s–70s): Southern redneck; racist, abusive and mean. Ruth Ann's grandfather.

TIME

The present.

SETTING

The Bean family home and surrounding swampland in fictitious Sugar Bean, Florida.

THE SUGAR WITCH was originally produced by Northside Theatre Company in San Jose, CA, 2007. It was directed by Richard T. Orlando. The cast was as follows:

SISSER	Kezia Radke
RUTH ANN MEEKS	JeannieRae Orlando
ANNABELLE	Kendra Owens
MOSES BEAN	Scott Cox
HANK HARTLEY	Paul Ulloa
GRANDDADDY MEEKS	Jerry Hitchcock

For Brian

ACT ONE

Scene One

*(**MUSIC:** "A Widow's Toast" by Neko Case.)*

*(**AT RISE**: the exterior house front and surrounding swampland of the Bean family homestead in Sugar Bean, Florida is revealed.)*

(In recent years, the 100 year-old house has fallen into a state of disrepair. The wood porch that wraps around the front of the house is decaying and appears to be sinking into the boggy ground. A marshy path winds its way from the old house through an ancient and haunted place that is known to the residents of Sugar Bean as Buster Swamp. An air of sadness engulfs the house. Dying stalks of sugarcane have toppled over and are rotting on the poisoned ground.)

(Stage-right of the house, hidden from view of the audience, is the venerable Watchalahoochee River.)

(A small "cane house" sits stage-left, although we only see the side and back, not the front and entrance. There is a small woodpile with a chopping block and ax nestled against the wall of the work shack.)

(A ceremonial "fire pit" can be found near the old cane house. The yard is scattered with old citrus packing crates. The crates may be used as chairs during the staging of the play. An old swing, a chair, and an antique rocker line up along the porch near the front screen door.)

*(Sitting on the porch in a large antique wheelchair is **SISSER**, an obese woman in her 40's. **SISSER** sits, staring off in the direction of the swamp. She unwraps a Little Debbie Star Crunch snack cake from its cellophane*

wrapper and begins to eat it slowly, relishing every bite. When she is finished, she unwraps another one. It is late afternoon.)

*(From out of the swamp, a young woman appears. She is in her late 20's–late 30's and wears a dress that seems to have been made some time in the 1940's. Her stringy hair is tied up with ribbon in the form of a large blue bow. Her make-up seems rather exaggerated, like a little girl playing dress-up. The woman's name is **RUTH ANN MEEKS**. She hides in the sugar cane field, watching the house and **SISSER** from a safe distance. As she attempts to get a better view of the porch, **RUTH ANN** inadvertently kicks over a rusty bucket, causing a commotion in the swamp.)*

SISSER. *(Calling from the porch)* Who's that in the sugarcane field?

RUTH ANN. *(Stepping into view)* I come to see Moses Bean.

*(**SISSER** takes another bite of her Star Crunch.)*

You his Mama?

SISSER. No.

RUTH ANN. Who are you then?

SISSER. *(After a pause)* Sisser.

RUTH ANN. Sisser?! What kind of stupid-ass name is that?

SISSER. It's what they call me.

(A shadow or peculiar light quickly flashes behind the front screen door.)

RUTH ANN. I need to speak with Moses Bean.

SISSER. He ain't home.

RUTH ANN. Then how come I just seen somebody traipse across back there behind that screen door?

SISSER. *(After a pause)* We got ghosts.

RUTH ANN. I don't believe in ghosts.

SISSER. *(After a pause)* Moses ain't home.

RUTH ANN. Now, how come you sitting up there big as you please in that wheelchair telling me fibs?

(**SISSER** *takes another bite of her snack cake.*)

RUTH ANN. *(cont'd)* I got me a right mind to go inside that house and hunt for Moses Bean myself.

(**ANNABELLE**, *an African-American woman in her late 40's, enters from the direction of the Watchalahoochee River. She carries a sack over her shoulder. She places it inside a small wooden boat that is sitting at the edge of the swamp. The boat is painted black and red and is covered in strange, ancient symbols. Standing at the edge of the swamp,* **ANNABELLE** *sees* **RUTH ANN**.)

ANNABELLE. *(To* **RUTH ANN***)* What you needin'?

RUTH ANN. You the maid?

ANNABELLE. State your business.

RUTH ANN. Moses Bean asked me to come by here and see him this afternoon. I walked all the way from town through that dark and evil swamp. *(After a pause)* And to top it off…I went and tore my good church dress on a jagged stalk of sugarcane. See… ?

(**RUTH ANN** *shows* **ANNABELLE** *and* **SISSER** *a tear in the hem of her dress.*)

My granddaddy's gonna beat me alive when he sees what's become of my good church dress. You need to set fire to that awful dead field out there.

ANNABELLE. You should count your blessings. Lots worse could've happened to you out there in Buster Swamp.

RUTH ANN. What you mean?

ANNABELLE. If them flying cats had seen you out there… they would've swooped down and tore you to pieces.

RUTH ANN. There ain't no such of a thing as flying cats.

ANNABELLE. Suit yourself.

RUTH ANN. I would appreciate it if one of you would go inside that house and let Moses Bean know that Ruth Ann Meeks is here.

ANNABELLE. Moses ain't home.

RUTH ANN. I know there's somebody hiding in that house.

ANNABELLE. We got ghosts.

(RUTH ANN crosses to the boat. She rocks it back and forth with her foot.)

RUTH ANN. *(To ANNABELLE)* This here your boat…?

ANNABELLE. What you wanna know for?

RUTH ANN. Just wondering, is all. *(After a pause)* You're Annabelle, ain't you?

(ANNABELLE is silent.)

My Granddaddy Meeks said you're some kind of witch woman. He said this whole place is cursed. Granddaddy Meeks said this house was built on an old Indian burial mound. He warned me not to come here but I didn't listen.

(RUTH ANN takes a step closer.)

Granddaddy Meeks said there was witches even before you that lived out here in this old Bean house. Sugar Witches. That's what he called 'em. *(After a pause)* Is that what you are? A sugar witch?

ANNABELLE. *(After a pause)* Moses ain't here.

RUTH ANN. Granddaddy Meeks said you got powers and such. He said sugar witches can make potions out of cane syrup. Is that what you do?

(ANNABELLE is silent.)

Granddaddy Meeks said you could see inside a locked box if you wanted to. I don't believe any of that foolishness myself. But if it were true…that means you could look right through my pocket book and tell what's in it.

ANNABELLE. *(After a pause)* A piece of gum, a red tube of lipstick, a miniature Bible, and a pink pair of underdrawers.

RUTH ANN. *(Stunned)* How'd you do that?! That's some kind of trick, ain't it?

ANNABELLE. It's gonna be getting dark soon…and it's a long walk back to town. So I suggest you get on your way. You don't want to be caught in Buster Swamp after sundown.

(**RUTH ANN** *sits on an old crate in the front yard.*)

RUTH ANN. *(Defiantly)* I think I'll just set myself down right here and get comfortable till Moses Bean comes home.

ANNABELLE. You might be waiting a while.

RUTH ANN. That's all right with me. Moses Bean can drive me back into Sugar Bean in that nice pick-up truck of his. *(After a pause)* You got any sweet tea?

(**ANNABELLE** *opens the screen door and disappears inside the house. The screen door slams shut behind her.*)

SISSER. That's a nice ribbon you got yourself.

RUTH ANN. *(Touching her hair ribbon)* Ain't it?

SISSER. *(After a pause)* You got real pretty hair...

RUTH ANN. Don't I?

(**RUTH ANN** *proudly touches the ribbon, then begins to twirl her hair with her fingers.*)

SISSER. Where did you get a pretty ribbon like that?

RUTH ANN. It was a present.

SISSER. From a man friend?

RUTH ANN. *(Exaggerating)* Oh, I got me dozens of boyfriends.

SISSER. Your boyfriends take you to the picture show?

RUTH ANN. They sure do. *(After a pause)* But I can't go to any more movies after tomorrow.

SISSER. How come?

RUTH ANN. I'm getting baptized in the Watchalahoochee River.

SISSER. What you gonna do that for?

RUTH ANN. So all my sins will get washed away. *(After a pause)* Ain't you been baptized?

SISSER. No, ma'am.

RUTH ANN. Then you're gonna burn in hell.

SISSER. No, I ain't. I'm gonna be in heaven with my Mama and my Daddy. Annabelle said so.

RUTH ANN. *(Crossing closer to **SISSER**)* The Devil's gonna toast you like a marshmallow on a stick. *(After a pause)* How come you so big and fat?

SISSER. *(After a pause)* I don't know.

RUTH ANN. How much food you eat? *(Taking in **SISSER**'s size)* I bet you weigh a thousand pounds.

*(**SISSER** hides a Star Crunch under her leg.)*

That's a homemade dress, ain't it?

SISSER. Annabelle made it.

RUTH ANN. She make all your clothes?

SISSER. Yeah.

RUTH ANN. This dress I got on belonged to my Great Grandma Meeks. Great Grandma Meeks has been dead a long, long time. She drowned in the flood. Today's the anniversary. Did you know that?

SISSER. *(Ignoring the question)* What you want with my brother?

RUTH ANN. *(Walking away from **SISSER**)* Why you think I'd tell you? You're just a big fat heifer sitting up on a porch in a nasty-ass dress some nigger made you.

(There is the sudden sound of a bass chord – almost like the hum of an electrical current. The windows of the old Bean house begin to glow a deep blood red, almost as if the house itself were alive and growing angry. Like a heartbeat, the red light pulsates through the windows and behind the front screen door. The sound continues.)

RUTH ANN. *(cont'd)* *(Growing frightened)* What is that?

SISSER. What?

RUTH ANN. That. That…sound.

SISSER. I don't hear nothing.

*(**RUTH ANN** does not look behind her at the house – she doesn't see the glowing red windows. Suddenly the sound stops and the lights return to normal.)*

SISSER. *(cont'd) (After a pause)* Can I see your Bible? The one Annabelle said you got in your pocket book?

RUTH ANN. *(Opening her purse)* It's a little Bible…small enough to fit in your purse…or the pocket of your dress. That way…the Lord is always with you. *(After a pause)* That's what the Reverend Buddy Tifton said.

(**RUTH ANN** *slips the Bible in the front pocket of her threadbare print dress.*)

SISSER. *(Reaching her hand out)* Let me hold it a minute…

RUTH ANN. I don't want you touching it. You might ruin it somehow…get nasty fat-germs on it.

SISSER. I ain't gonna ruin it. I'm just gonna hold it.

RUTH ANN. I'll sell it to you.

SISSER. I ain't got no money.

RUTH ANN. Granddaddy Meeks said the Bean family used to own this whole entire town of Sugar Bean. That's where it got its name. You are a Bean, ain't you?

SISSER. Yeah.

RUTH ANN. Well, then…you know you got money so if you want this cute little Bible…you best hand over some cash.

SISSER. How much you want for it?

RUTH ANN. How much is it worth to you?

SISSER. Twenty-five cent.

(**RUTH ANN** *starts laughing.*)

RUTH ANN. Twenty-five cent?! Girl, you must be crazy. This here Bible is worth way more than twenty-five cent!

SISSER. I'll give you a dollar for it.

RUTH ANN. *(After a pause)* Now that I've had me a real good look at you…I wouldn't sell you this Bible not for a million dollars.

(*The screen door opens and* **ANNABELLE** *enters, carrying a glass of iced tea. She crosses to* **RUTH ANN** *and offers her the drink.*)

ANNABELLE. Here.

(**RUTH ANN** *takes the glass from* **ANNABELLE** *and sits back down on the crate in the front yard.*)

RUTH ANN. *(Looking inside the glass)* How do I know you ain't put something nasty in it?

(**RUTH ANN** *turns the glass over and pours the tea in the dirt.*)

SISSER. *(To* **ANNABELLE***)* That gal done went and poured her tea out in the dirt.

RUTH ANN. I think I'd prefer to have me some lemonade.

(**RUTH ANN** *raises the empty glass above her head. Suddenly, the spot where* **RUTH ANN** *is sitting begins to glow red.* **RUTH ANN** *suddenly screams out in pain, dropping the glass as if it were on fire.*)

ANNABELLE. *(Slight smile)* Burn yourself?

RUTH ANN. What'd you do to that glass?!

(*Suddenly we hear the sounds of winged animals flying over the house.*)

RUTH ANN. *(cont'd)* What's that sound? Is that birds?

ANNABELLE. No. Ain't birds.

(*The terrible sound of the flying cats echoes through the swamp.*

RUTH ANN *crosses down-stage. She looks up in the air.*)

RUTH ANN. What are those terrible things?!

ANNABELLE. Flying cats. But you said you don't believe in them. Remember?

RUTH ANN. I see 'em! I see 'em flying and circling like buzzards! *(To* **ANNABELLE***)* What kind of evil you bringing, witch?!

ANNABELLE. Them cats been here for millions of years. They ain't evil.

RUTH ANN. Why do they keep circling around like that?!

ANNABELLE. I reckon they see something they want.

RUTH ANN. *(Cowering)* Do they eat people?!

ANNABELLE. *(Having some fun)* Oh, that's a big treat for them. They'll swoop down on you and carry you off to their lair in the swamp. That way they can eat on you for days and days before you die and turn to rot.

*(Screaming at the top of her lungs, **RUTH ANN** makes a sudden dash for the swamp.)*

SISSER. *(Laughing)* Did you see the way that gal took off running?

ANNABELLE. *(Flatly)* Yeah. I seen it.

SISSER. I think she's crazy. What do you think, Annabelle?

ANNABELLE. She ain't got all that's coming to her, that's for sure.

SISSER. You think she's gonna run all the way back to town?

ANNABELLE. I'm gonna go and follow her…make sure she gets out of the swamp in one piece.

*(**ANNABELLE** descends the steps of the porch and exits through the sugarcane field.)*

*(**SISSER** begins to sing "What a Friend We Have In Jesus," then picks up a box that is sitting on the table beside her wheelchair. She opens the lid and peers inside, then quickly closes it again.)*

*(After a few moments, we hear the sound of an approaching vehicle as it makes its way down the long dirt road leading to the house. This is followed by the sound of a car door opening and closing. **MOSES BEAN**, a handsome young man in his mid–late 20's enters from the sugarcane field. He is dressed in a plain work shirt and faded jeans. Carrying a bag of groceries, **MOSES** crosses to **SISSER** on the porch.)*

MOSES. Hey, Sisser.

SISSER. What'd you bring me?

MOSES. Your favorites…

*(**MOSES** removes a carton of Little Debbie snack cakes from the bag and hands the box to his sister.)*

SISSER. Oatmeal cream pies…*(looking disappointed)* You didn't get me no Star Crunches…?

(**MOSES** *removes the box of Star Crunches from the bag.*)

MOSES. I figured I'd put these up in the pantry for later.

(**SISSER** *grabs the second box from* **MOSES**, *tears it open and removes one of the snack cakes from inside.*)

SISSER. I want 'em right here so I don't have to get up and go huntin' for 'em.

(**SISSER** *sets the boxes down on the small table next to her wheelchair.*)

MOSES. Like you'd get up and go huntin' for 'em. You know good and damn well I'm the one that would have to bring 'em to you.

(**MOSES** *vanishes inside the house with the grocery bags.*)

(From inside the house) Where's Annabelle?

SISSER. She went to run off this crazy gal that come here looking for you.

MOSES. *(Returning to the porch)* What crazy gal?

SISSER. *(Chewing her snack cake)* She had a pretty blue bow in her hair. And a cute little Bible.

MOSES. Her name Ruth Ann Meeks?

SISSER. Does this gal you're talking about have a pretty blue ribbon in her hair?

MOSES. I can't think of anyone else it could be. *(After a pause)* That goddamn girl is driving me crazy.

(**MOSES** *sits down on the top step of the porch.*)

SISSER. *(After a pause)* Did you fix a lot of engines today, Brother?

MOSES. *(Tired)* Yes, ma'am…I sure did.

(**SISSER** *picks up the box and holds it in her lap.*)

SISSER. Something bad happened to Lurlene, the Palmetto bug.

MOSES. What?

SISSER. She up and died on me.

MOSES. Something like that's to be expected when you consider the fact that palmetto bugs don't have that long a life span.

SISSER. She was my favorite in the whole collection. *(After a pause)* I think Annabelle killed her.

MOSES. *(Not believing her)* Now, why would Annabelle do something like that?

SISSER. Just full of meanness, I reckon.

MOSES. Annabelle wouldn't kill none of your bugs and you know it.

SISSER. We need to give Lurlene, the Palmetto Bug, a proper burial.

MOSES. She's just a bug.

SISSER. Here…

(**SISSER** *holds up a match box.*)

SISSER. *(cont'd)* I put her in this little matchbox.

MOSES. Any special place you want me to dig?

SISSER. Over by the well. They like to be around water.

(**MOSES** *takes the box from his sister. He then crosses to the cane house and grabs a shovel.*)

SISSER. *(cont'd) (After a pause)* We should sing a hymn or something, don't you think?

MOSES. Look. I'll bury her. But I ain't serenading no goddamn bug.

(**MOSES** *begins to dig a hole in the ground near the old well. As he digs,* **SISSER** *begins to sing "Shall We Gather At The River." Moses quickly buries the small matchbox coffin, then covers it with dirt.*)

MOSES *(cont'd)* There. Done.

(**MOSES** *returns the shovel to the cane house.*)

SISSER. What about a grave marker?

(MOSES crosses to the wood pile, takes some twigs and string and quickly fashions a makeshift cross. He makes his way downstage to the old well.)

SISSER. *(Sadly)* Good-bye, Lurlene…you were a good bug.

MOSES. She's a dead bug now.

SISSER. I ain't got all that many left in the collection. I'm really gonna miss Lurlene.

MOSES. I don't know how you can even tell 'em apart. They all look the same to me. One bug looks like any other.

(MOSES places the cross on Lurlene's grave.)

SISSER. *(After a pause)* You think something bad's happened to Annabelle out in the swamp?

MOSES. Annabelle can take care of herself.

SISSER. *(Chewing)* I can't decide whether I like the oatmeal cream pies better or the Star Crunches. *(After a pause)* It's a toss up.

MOSES. When Annabelle comes back…I want you to go in the house and have her help you pick out one of your nice dresses.

SISSER. What for?

MOSES. *(Smiling)* We're having company for supper. I've invited this real nice fellow I know from down at the Texaco. He brings his work vehicle into the shop and I service it for him. *(After a pause)* We need to start being more social.

SISSER. What you making for dinner?

MOSES. Chicken and Dumplings.

SISSER. What's gonna go with it?

MOSES. You'll see when I set the plate down in front of you.

*(**ANNABELLE** enters from the swamp.)*

SISSER. There's Annabelle.

ANNABELLE. *(To **MOSES**)* I need to speak with you.

MOSES. What is it?

ANNABELLE. That gal that come here looking for you...

MOSES. I don't even hardly know her. She comes down to the Texaco and stands around all day...just staring at me...trying to make conversation. *(After a pause)* Gives me the creeps.

SISSER. I gotta go to the bathroom.

*(**ANNABELLE** crosses to the porch. She opens the screen door and pushes **SISSER**'s wheelchair inside the house.)*

*(**MOSES** crosses to the woodpile and begins to chop some wood for the fire pit.)*

*(**RUTH ANN MEEKS** enters from the sugarcane field, holding her Bible in her hand.)*

RUTH ANN. *(Seductively)* Moses Bean...I been huntin' you.

MOSES. What are you doing here? I don't recall giving you an invitation.

RUTH ANN. Yes, you did. I seen the way you was looking at me when I was down at the shop watching you work on that old man's truck.

MOSES. I wasn't looking at you.

RUTH ANN. I took off my shoe and was diggin' my toes in the dirt like this...*(she kicks off her shoe and demonstrates)* and when I looked up...I caught you looking at my foot.

MOSES. *(After a pause)* You're out of your cotton-picking mind.

RUTH ANN. *(Seductively)* You wanna see me naked, Moses Bean?

MOSES. You need to go home, is what you need to do.

*(**MOSES** moves away from **RUTH ANN**.)*

RUTH ANN. I'm getting baptized tomorrow morning.

MOSES. So, what's that got to do with me?

RUTH ANN. I got one more night to do something sinful.

MOSES. You're crazy.

RUTH ANN. We can go off in that sugarcane field right now and have sinful relations. And then come tomorrow...

when I get baptized in the river…all my sins will be washed away and I can start my life anew.

MOSES. You need to go, is what you need to do. And quit coming down to my place of work. You're gonna keep on till you get me fired.

RUTH ANN. Why you being so mean?

MOSES. How many times do I have to tell you to stay the hell away from me?

RUTH ANN. *(Suddenly, with great fury)* I'll show you!

(In a fit of rage, RUTH ANN picks up the cross from Lurlene's grave and pounds it against the dirt, almost breaking it.)

MOSES. You quit that right now!

(MOSES grabs RUTH ANN's arm and takes the cross away from her.)

RUTH ANN. What you gonna do, now, Moses Bean? Beat me?

MOSES. You get off my property.

RUTH ANN. *(Furious)* I'll tell Granddaddy Meeks you took advantage of me. You'll be sorry then, Moses Bean!

(Suddenly, the sounds of the flying cats can be heard high above the haunted swamp.)

RUTH ANN. *(Frightened)* That's them come back!

(RUTH ANN sees ANNABELLE standing in the doorway.)

RUTH ANN. *(cont'd)* It's that Sugar Witch's doing!

MOSES. You best get running then!

(RUTH ANN screams and runs for the swamp. ANNABELLE crosses to MOSES in the yard.)

ANNABELLE. I got a feeling we ain't seen the last of her.

MOSES. Should I follow after her? Make sure she gets out of the swamp?

ANNABELLE. If we're lucky – she'll step foot inside a gator's ass and then we won't have to worry about her.

MOSES. You should've heard the crazy talk coming out of that girl's mouth.

ANNABELLE. She's trouble come knocking at the door.

MOSES. Well, I better get inside and start supper. We got company coming over tonight.

ANNABELLE. Sisser said as much.

MOSES. You'll like him, Annabelle. He's a really nice fellow.

ANNABELLE. What's his name?

MOSES. Hank. Hank Hartley. For the last few months… he's been coming down to the Texaco. He brings his work vehicle in at least once a week. Even when there's nothing wrong with it. *(After a pause)* He brings it in just to have me look at it and make sure everything's okay. And he always leaves me a really good tip…even when I don't have to fix anything.

(MOSES makes his way up the porch steps.)

I just thought it might be a good idea if we start having some company. For Sisser's sake more than anything else.

ANNABELLE. You think having visitors over is gonna make any difference to Sisser?

MOSES. It might. You never know.

ANNABELLE. Well, I ain't got the same faith as you do when it comes to her.

MOSES. *(After a pause)* Sometimes…I get to thinking that it might really be true.

ANNABELLE. What's that?

MOSES. The mark. The mark the Sugar Witch put on the Bean Family all those years ago.

ANNABELLE. You know what today is?

MOSES. No. What?

ANNABELLE. It's the anniversary of the hurricane that come through…and the Great Flood.

MOSES. No wonder the curse has been on my mind all day.

ANNABELLE. You can feel it in your bones. I feel it, too. That's when it all started. All those years ago...long before you and me was even born.

(**ANNABELLE** *peers out into the dark swamp.*)

The spirits of the dead will walk the swamp tonight. Pray morning comes soon, Moses Bean. (*After a pause*) Even Sisser feels it... she don't know it... but she feels it anyway. It's a knowing... even without knowing.

MOSES. I'm glad Mama never lived long enough to see what's become of Sisser. (*After a pause*) I've tried, Annabelle. I've tried to make a good life for her. But whatever I do...it dies...just like that sugarcane field out there.

(**ANNABELLE** *crosses over to* **MOSES**. *She touches his shoulder with her hand.*)

ANNABELLE. Your mama would be proud of you, Moses.

MOSES. You're just saying that.

ANNABELLE. Your mama loves you.

MOSES. You talk like she's still alive.

ANNABELLE. She is. Look around... she's in the swamp... in the trees... she's in the wood that holds up this very porch, shaky as it is. She watches out for you, Moses. She protects you and Sisser. And don't you ever doubt it. Why you think you've both survived the curse this long? (*After a pause*) No, sir. There ain't a place in Buster Swamp where your mama's spirit don't dwell.

MOSES. (*After a pause*) Do you believe it? Do you believe we're really marked?

ANNABELLE. (*Turning away*) Don't matter what I believe.

MOSES. I can't tell you how many times I've thought of leaving this godforsaken place.

ANNABELLE. Then why don't you? You're a free man. Pack up your things, Moses Bean. Get in your truck and head on up the road.

MOSES. You know I can't do that. I gotta stay here and look after Sisser. She's helpless...she'd never make it on her own.

(From inside the house we hear Sisser's voice.)

SISSER. *(O.S.)* Annabelle?! My chair's hung up on the rug! My wheel's stuck and I can't move!

*(**ANNABELLE** crosses to the screen door.)*

MOSES. We got any sugar brew out in the cane house? It might be nice to open a bottle and share it with Hank after supper.

ANNABELLE. There's a few bottles left.

*(**ANNABELLE** turns and crosses to the front door. **MOSES** stops her just as she opens the screen door.)*

MOSES. Annabelle?

ANNABELLE. Yeah?

MOSES. *(After a pause)* Do you believe we're cursed?

*(**ANNABELLE** gives no answer.)*

ANNABELLE. I need to see about Sisser.

MOSES. I need to know.

ANNABELLE. *(After a pause)* Yes, Moses Bean. I believe so.

(The lights dim. End of Scene One.)

Scene Two

*(**MUSIC:** "Butterfly's Day Out" by Yo-Yo Ma [from Appalachia Waltz"])*

*(An hour later. **SISSER** is sitting on the front porch in her wheelchair, staring off into the swamp. She is wearing a different dress. **ANNABELLE** sits on the porch in the old rocking chair.)*

SISSER. I think that gal with the blue bow in her hair got inside the house somehow when I weren't looking and killed my bug.

ANNABELLE. *(Humoring her)* Oh, is that what you think?

SISSER. Something's gotta be done about it.

ANNABELLE. Oh, and what's that?

SISSER. *(Opening another snack cake)* I ain't sure just yet. I'm gonna need me some more time to think on it.

ANNABELLE. *(Sarcastically)* Well, when you figure it out make sure you let me know. *(Enjoying this)* We can have a party…ring some bells…sing some songs…light a fire…dance all night in the sugarcane field.

SISSER. *(Holding up a snack cake)* You want a Star Crunch?

ANNABELLE. Now you're just trying to get in my good graces.

*(**SISSER** rips open the cellophane and takes a bite of the snack cake.)*

*(**ANNABELLE** descends the steps of the porch and makes her way across the yard.)*

SISSER. Where you going?

ANNABELLE. Out to the cane house. I gotta get us some Sugar Brew for tonight.

SISSER. We got any more sugar wine?

ANNABELLE. You don't need to be drinkin'. The last time you drank…you stood in the bathroom half the night…looking at yourself in the mirror and cryin'. Brought the whole mood of the house down.

(ANNABELLE *exits to the cane house. After a few moments, there is the sound of an approaching vehicle coming towards the house down the long, winding swamp road.*)

SISSER. (*Calling to* ANNABELLE) Somebody's coming up the road!

(*As the sound of the approaching car grows louder,* SISSER *peers into the distance, trying to get a better look at what is coming up the road. Suddenly,* SISSER *begins to scream bloody murder. She wails and beats at her chest with her fists. She is absolutely terrified by what she sees coming towards her.*)

SISSER. (*cont'd*) (*Screaming*) Death wagon...death wagon...death wagon...!

(MOSES *comes running out of the house, rushing to* SISSER'*s side.* ANNABELLE *comes out of the cane house to see what all the fuss is about.*)

MOSES. (*Attempting to calm* SISSER) What's the matter with you?! Why you screaming like that?!

ANNABELLE. (*Standing in the front yard*) What's she carrying on about?!

(SISSER *points off-stage in the direction of the swamp road.*)

SISSER. (*In hysterics*) It's a death wagon come for me!

MOSES. That's my friend...Hank Hartley...

ANNABELLE. (*Looking at the approaching car*) What's he driving that for?

MOSES. He works down at the funeral home.

SISSER. (*Still crying*) It's the death wagon come for me, I know it!

MOSES. (*Pleading for help*) Annabelle... .?

ANNABELLE. (*Crossing up to the porch*) I'll take her in the house. (*To* SISSER) Look how you got yourself all worked up for nothing.

*(As **ANNABELLE** pushes **SISSER**'s wheelchair through the screen door, **SISSER** continues crying about the "death wagon.")*

ANNABELLE *(O.S.) (cont'd)* Ain't no death wagon coming for you…so you just calm yourself down and quit all this carrying on. You acting like a big baby…

*(**ANNABELLE** and **SISSER** disappear inside the house.)*

*(**MOSES** fixes his hair in the reflection of the window, then quickly descends the steps of the porch.)*

*(**HANK HARTLEY**, a handsome man in his mid to late 30's, enters from the swamp. He is carrying a brown paper bag. The two men shake hands.)*

HANK. I heard quite a commotion as I was driving up. Everything alright?

MOSES. I'm afraid my sister got a little upset when she saw you drive up. It's not everyday she sees a funeral car pull up to the house.

HANK. I couldn't get my car started so I decided to take the hearse. I'm sorry if I upset your sister.

MOSES. My sister tends to be a little high strung…even under the best of circumstances.

*(**HANK** removes a bottle of whiskey from the brown paper bag.)*

HANK. I hope you don't mind…but I brought us a little libation.

MOSES. *(Taking the bottle)* I told you not to bring anything.

HANK. I know. I just thought we might want a little drink before supper. And besides…I just can't bring myself to show up anywhere empty-handed.

MOSES. Thank you, Hank. That was very nice of you.

HANK. Oh, it was the least I could do.

MOSES. Well…come on up on the porch. Watch your step, though…this porch ain't in the best of shape, I'm afraid.

HANK. *(Looking up at the house)* I just love these old Florida houses. This sure is a wonderful place you have, Moses.

(The two men climb the steps to the porch.)

MOSES. My great grandfather, Buster Bean, built this porch with sunsets in mind.

*(**MOSES** seems a little nervous and unsure of himself. He is not used to entertaining.)*

HANK. Is it haunted?

MOSES. Oh, it's haunted alright. Used to scare the living daylights out of me when I was a kid. It's funny how you grow out of things.

HANK. You're a braver man than me, Moses Bean.

MOSES. Listen to you! You work in a funeral home. This old house is nothing compared to that place.

(The two men stand at the porch railing, looking off into the distance.)

MOSES. *(cont'd)* Looks like we're gonna have a pretty sunset.

HANK. You can even see the river from here.

MOSES. If you want…before dinner…we can ask Annabelle if she'll take us out in the boat. *(Gazing at the river)* We still got an hour or so of daylight, at least.

HANK. I don't get out on the river as much as I should. *(After a pause, looking at **MOSES**)* It sure is a beautiful sight.

*(**HANK** watches **MOSES**. His face is full of desire and longing for the younger man. **MOSES** smiles, then turns to face his friend. There is a moment of quiet connection between the two men; something unspoken.)*

MOSES. Do you fish, Hank?

HANK. No, I'm afraid I'm not much of a sportsman.

MOSES. Annabelle loves to fish. I've never cared for it all that much myself. I don't even like to stick a hook through a worm.

(**HANK** *laughs softly.*)

MOSES. *(cont'd)* But I do enjoy the river. In fact…my very first memory is of the river.

HANK. So it's just you and your sister, now? Your parents are gone?

MOSES. My dad run off and left the family years ago. In fact, I don't even remember him. My sister was fourteen years old when I come along. So there's a big age difference between the two of us.

HANK. And your mother?

MOSES. She died when I was little. But I have memories of her. She had a wonderful laugh. Sometimes…late at night…when I can't sleep…I swear I hear Mama's laughter coming from somewhere deep inside that house.

HANK. Ghosts?

MOSES. Ghosts. *(After a pause)* So it's just me and Sisser. And Annabelle. Annabelle's been here as long as I can remember. She raised me after Mama died. I don't know what Sisser and I would've done without Annabelle. She ain't a Bean, of course. But…she's family.

HANK. *(Looking off in the distance; after a pause)* Yes, sir…this sure is a beautiful place. You're a lucky man, Moses Bean. A very lucky man.

(**ANNABELLE** *opens the screen door and joins the men on the porch. She is carrying a tray with a pitcher of iced tea and three drinking glasses.*)

ANNABELLE. Y'all boys care for some iced tea?

(**MOSES** *takes the tray from* **ANNABELLE** *and sets it down in the yard on an old crate.*)

MOSES. Hank…this is Annabelle. Annabelle…Hank Hartley.

(**HANK** *and* **ANNABELLE** *shake hands.*)

HANK. It's a pleasure to meet you, ma'am.

ANNABELLE. Pleasure's mine.

(**ANNABELLE** *turns* **HANK***'s hand over and silently reads his palm, softly touching the lines with her fingers. Finally, she releases his hand, then turns her attention to the tea.*)

ANNABELLE *(cont'd)* This tea comes from a special brew I gathered myself out in the swamp. It's been known to work as a love potion. *(Gazing at* **HANK***; suggestively)* You like sweet tea, Mr. Hartley?

HANK. It's my favorite, in fact. And please...call me Hank. Everybody does.

(**HANK** *looks at* **MOSES** *and smiles.*)

(**ANNABELLE** *stares at* **HANK** *for a moment, then turns her gaze to* **MOSES**. **MOSES** *is staring at* **HANK**, *a big love-struck smile on his face. He looks like a teenager experiencing his first crush.* **ANNABELLE** *registers the attraction. Her eyes say everything. She then reaches for the pitcher.*)

MOSES. *(To* **ANNABELLE***)* I'll do that. Y'all sit down and just relax.

(**ANNABELLE** *sits down in the rocking chair and props her feet up on an old crate.* **MOSES** *pours a glass of tea, spilling some on the table.*)

MOSES. *(cont'd)* Now, look at what I've done?! I don't know what's come over me. I ain't usually this clumsy.

ANNABELLE. *(To* **HANK***)* Moses is a dreamer...always got his mind far away from where it ought to be.

MOSES. *(To* **ANNABELLE***; playfully)* You're one to talk.

(**MOSES** *rushes into the house to get something to clean up the spill.*)

ANNABELLE. I ain't saying there's something wrong with it. I'm just stating a fact. *(To* **HANK***)* He's just like his Mama when it comes to being a daydreamer.

MOSES. *(Re-enters with a kitchen towel)* I pay the bills.

(**MOSES** *cleans up the spill.*)

ANNABELLE. I ain't finding fault. I'm just making a comment. *(After a pause)* Now, Sisser...Lord have mercy... I don't even know what to say about Sisser.

HANK. *(To ANNABELLE)* I'm sorry I upset Miss Bean with my arrival. As I was explaining to Moses...my car wouldn't start this afternoon...

ANNABELLE. *(To HANK)* Oh, Sisser'll be alright. I told her if she calms down and behaves herself...she can come out and visit with us on the porch.

MOSES. Where is Sisser?

ANNABELLE. *(Taking the glass)* In the bathroom. Washing her face.

MOSES. Hank...my sister is...well, she's a little...different from most people.

HANK. I'm sure your sister's a lovely person, Moses.

(MOSES hands ANNABELLE her tea.)

ANNABELLE. She's spoiled rotten, is what she is. *(To MOSES)* I told 'em they was gonna rue the day they raised her like they done. Letting her have her way all the time...giving her everything she always wanted...not cutting her off at the dinner table when they should have. *(To HANK)* I tell you...that girl eats like a workin' man!

MOSES. *(Slightly embarrassed)* Sisser's always had a very...substantial appetite.

HANK. Well, we all love to eat. I know I do.

MOSES. *(Handing HANK his glass of iced-tea)* Here you go, Hank...

HANK. *(Taking the glass)* Thank you. Now, this should hit the spot.

(MOSES and HANK both take a drink of the tea in unison. ANNABELLE watches from the porch. She waits to see HANK's reaction to the tea.)

HANK. *(cont'd) (After a pause; smiling)* Wonderful. Just wonderful. That is fine tea, Miss Annabelle.

(Pleased that her tea is such a hit, ANNABELLE smiles

broadly.)

MOSES. *(To* **ANNABELLE***)* Hank brought us some whiskey.

ANNABELLE. Well, hell…if I had known that I wouldn't have made the tea!

HANK. Miss Annabelle…I saw your signs out on the main road as I was driving up here this afternoon. You do a good business?

ANNABELLE. Oh, I can't complain. But…business ain't what it used to be, that's for sure. Now, I do have some regular costumers that come by. The sugar brew is still popular…and the potions…and the herbs…all good sellers.

MOSES. *(To* **HANK***)* Mrs. Hurst brought her little baby boy by here last week…

ANNABELLE. Thrush mouth. Terrible thing for a baby to have. Just hurts its little mouth something fierce. Thrush-mouth cry out of a little baby is just plum terrible. *(After a pause)* It'll send chills up the crack or your ass.

*(***HANK*** starts to laugh.)*

HANK. Now, that's a real interesting way of putting it.

MOSES. You should've seen it, Hank. Annabelle took that little baby out in the swamp and cured him. And all she had with her was some herbs.

ANNABELLE. And the Bible…don't forget the Bible.

MOSES. Even a doctor can't do that.

HANK. That's a remarkable gift, Miss Annabelle.

ANNABELLE. Or a curse. I still ain't figured out which. *(After a pause)* What I know…I learned from my mama… and she learned it from her mama…and so on through the years all the way back to the Ancients.

HANK. A very long tradition. That's something to be proud of. Tradition is important. My people have been in the funeral home business for several generations now. I never thought I'd go into the business but…well, you know how life can take a turn…and before you know it…*(sadly)* you wind up in a place you never thought you'd be.

MOSES. *(To* **ANNABELLE***; impressed)* Hank went off to Jacksonville to college. He's just come back to town. But he lived in the city for a long time. Didn't you, Hank?

HANK. It's strange being back in Sugar Bean. When I left this town at eighteen years of age…I swore I'd never come back. And here I am. Doing what I said I'd never do.

MOSES. I've never even been out of Sugar Bean in my whole entire life. I ain't even been to the Magic Kingdom.

HANK. Well, I'm sure you'll have that opportunity one day.

MOSES. Annabelle's been up the river all the way to the Indian Islands. Haven't you, Annabelle? I can't go 'cause I'm still a virgin. Ain't that right, Annabelle?

(**ANNABELLE** *smiles and drinks her tea.*)

HANK. *(Spitting out his tea)* I'm terribly sorry…I just…

MOSES. No, it's alright. I ain't ashamed to admit it. You can't be a virgin and go to the Indian Islands, ain't that right, Annabelle?

HANK. *(To* **ANNABELLE***)* Is that true, Miss Annabelle?

ANNABELLE. Sure is. Them Indians'll eat you if you're a virgin. No, sir. That island ain't safe for virgins.

MOSES. Annabelle says she'll take me with her as soon as I lose my virginity. All kinds of strange things happen on that island. It's where Annabelle gets some of her most powerful potions, ain't it, Annabelle?

HANK. I never even heard of the Indian Islands. *(Smiling; to* **MOSES***)* Are you sure she isn't pulling your leg? I mean, that sounds like a tall-tale to me.

ANNABELLE. You ain't heard nothing yet. You should hear how Moses got his name.

HANK. It's a righteous, handsome name. As a matter of fact, if I were to ever have a son of my own…I think I'd name him Moses, too.

(**ANNABELLE**, *a master storyteller, begins to set the*

stage.)

ANNABELLE. It's a strange story…but true.

MOSES. You ain't gonna tell that old story, now, are you?

ANNABELLE. It's a good story and besides…I was there. And since I seen it with my very own eyes… I reckon that gives me the right to tell it to anybody I want to.

HANK. Well, now you've really got me curious.

(MUSIC: Underscoring #1.)

ANNABELLE. It was late in the afternoon…about this time of day…and I was down at the edge of the Watchalahoochee River…washing my feet…and sunning myself…doing a little fishing…you know…just enjoying the day. When all of a sudden…a strong wind come up from the South…and I heard a voice in the wind…almost like a hymn. And just about that time… I looked up and there was a small boat floating all by itself down the river…coming towards me. I just figured it got away from its owner…or maybe its captain fell overboard and drowned in the river…or got eat by gators. So I drew near to investigate…and as I wadded out in the water I used a long stick to grab hold of it. And I pulled the boat over to me…and when I looked inside…there he was…a little baby boy…just a 'smiling up at me. So I grabbed him up out of the boat and I run all the way back here to the house to show Mrs. Bean what I had found. And when Mrs. Bean laid eyes on that child…she claimed him as her very own. We figured his real Mama must've abandoned him.

HANK. *(To* **ANNABELLE***)* Are you saying that little baby you found in the boat was Moses?

ANNABELLE. Not the Moses in the Bible. But the Moses of Sugar Bean. When I picked him up out of the boat… there was a little piece of paper safety pinned to his diaper. It said…"His name is Moses."

*(**MUSIC:** underscoring #1 ends.)*

HANK. That's the most incredible story I've ever heard in my life.

MOSES. *(With great pride)* Just like in the Bible. Ain't that something?

HANK. Maybe you're a prophet, too. Did you ever think of that?

MOSES. 'Cept I can't even get myself out of Sugar Bean let alone set the whole of Egypt free.

(Suddenly, there is the sound of the flying cats high above the swamp. **HANK** *looks up in the air, startled.)*

HANK. What on earth?!

ANNABELLE. That's the flying cats.

MOSES. They make a racket, don't they?

ANNABELLE. I don't like the way them cats been acting. I think it's the anniversary of the Great Flood that's got 'em all stirred up.

HANK. *(Not sure he's hearing right)* I'm sorry...did you say... flying cats?

MOSES. Yeah. They live out here in Buster Swamp.

HANK. What in the world is a flying cat?

MOSES. Just like what it sounds. It's a big, nasty bobcat-looking thing...'cept it's got wings...and fangs...and it flies in the air.

ANNABELLE. And walks the earth when it wants to. As far as anyone knows...they been here for thousands of years...

MOSES. Ever since the dinosaurs. They must've survived the ice age somehow.

HANK. Can you get close enough to get a good look at one?

ANNABELLE. I wouldn't, if I were you. They can be kind of ornery. Just last week...one of 'em stole away with a little baby right on the other side of Buster Swamp. *(After a pause)* Terrible tragedy that was.

MOSES. The poor Mama lost her mind. Had to go to a mental institution. Doctors don't think she'll ever be the same.

HANK. *(Laughs)* Okay...I know when my leg's being pulled.
MOSES. No, Hank. It's the truth. Annabelle can show you.

>   (**ANNABELLE** *descends the steps of the porch. She stares at* **HANK** *for a few moments, studying his face. After a moment,* **ANNABELLE** *crosses to the cane house and disappears inside the old work shack.*)

MOSES. *(cont'd) (To* **HANK***)* You ready?
HANK. *(A little nervous)* I don't know. Am I?

>   (**ANNABELLE** *appears from the cane house, carrying a glass aquarium covered with an old cloth. She sits the container down on a crate in the yard. She motions for* **HANK** *to sit down on the crate opposite the aquarium.* **HANK** *sits down,* **ANNABELLE** *motions for him to move closer. He reluctantly moves his crate closer to the mysterious container. Suspense hangs in the air.*)

MOSES. Go ahead, Annabelle. Let Hank see it.

>   (**ANNABELLE** *removes the white cloth to reveal a petrified flying cat inside the dusty glass aquarium. The long-dead creature housed inside is a hideous sight to behold.*)

HANK. *(Peering through the glass)* My God...it's got wings...
ANNABELLE. Ain't it something? My great grandmother caught this with her bare hands. Canned it herself. It come to me when my Mama died.
MOSES. Annabelle used to charge money for folks to come and look at it. Didn't you, Annabelle?
ANNABELLE. I had me some signs advertising it...up along the main road...going into town.
MOSES. But over time...the writing on 'em started to fade away...and we just never thought to put new ones up in their place.
ANNABELLE. Folks ain't as interested in things like flying cats anymore. At least...not like they used to be.
MOSES. The Reptile Woman offered Annabelle a hundred dollars...cash...if she'd sell it to her so she could put

it up on display at her Reptile Ranch on the other side of the swamp.

ANNABELLE. I told her I couldn't accept her offer. As tempting as it was. This flying cat is way too powerful to let anyone other than a sugar witch have possession of it.

MOSES. Sugar Witches have dominion over the flying cats. Ain't that right, Annabelle?

ANNABELLE. It's always been that way. And will be that way forever. Long after the last sugar witch dies.

MOSES. I just wish a man could become a sugar witch. Annabelle says she don't think it's possible, though.

HANK. How many sugar witches are left in the world?

(*A sadness suddenly falls over* **ANNABELLE** *and* **MOSES**.)

ANNABELLE. I'm the last of the sugar witches, I'm afraid. When I die… there's no more.

HANK. (*Sincerely*) I'm sorry to hear that, Miss Annabelle.

ANNABELLE. All things must come to an end. Even sugar witches.

MOSES. (*To* **HANK**; *smiling broadly*) Ain't Annabelle wise, Hank? I knew the two of you would get along just fine.

HANK. I'm afraid I don't know what to say. If I weren't standing here looking at it with my very own eyes… I'd never believe it. Flying cats…sugar witches…love potions…

MOSES. Tell him how it's supposed to end, Annabelle. (*Excited*) Tell Hank how a sugar witch has to leave the earth when her time is up. It's the saddest thing, Hank. Wait til you hear. Go on, Annabelle…tell Hank how it ends.

ANNABELLE. A sugar witch has to die by her own hand. It's been that way forever…all the way back to the Ancients.

(**ANNABELLE** *reaches inside her bag and removes a small purple bottle.*)

ANNABELLE. *(cont'd)* This is how I'll go. It's poison. I made it myself. Mama taught me how before she died and went to the Great Swamp beyond. Seven different swamp plants are used to make the potion.

(**ANNABELLE** *takes the cork out of the top and holds the bottle up for* **HANK** *to see. After a moment, he gently takes the bottle from* **ANNABELLE**.)

ANNABELLE. *(cont'd)* It's painless. You drink it all down… and in a few minutes…you fall into a death sleep. Never to wake again on this Earth.

(**ANNABELLE** *takes the bottle from* **HANK**.)

ANNABELLE. *(cont'd)* *(After a pause)* Never to wake again.

(**ANNABELLE** *places the bottle back inside her bag. After a moment,* **MOSES** *breaks the tension.*)

MOSES. Anybody care for some whiskey?

HANK. I could sure use some. Especially after looking inside that aquarium.

MOSES. Yeah. Me, too. We don't mean to bring you down, Hank…we just wanted to show you that it's real. It's all real. Every bit of it.

(**MOSES** *crosses to the porch and grabs the bottle of whiskey.*)

MOSES. *(cont'd)* I figure we'll just use our tea glasses. We might need more ice.

(**ANNABELLE** *notices* **SISSER**'s *wheelchair on the other side of the screen door.*)

ANNABELLE. You wanna come out and join us, Sisser?

SISSER. If you'll have me.

(**ANNABELLE** *starts to get up from her chair to help* **SISSER** *through the door only to have* **SISSER** *stop her.*)

SISSER. *(cont'd)* No. I want Brother to help me.

ANNABELLE. Suit yourself. I'll get more ice.

(**ANNABELLE** *opens the screen door and enters the house.*)

(MOSES gets up from his chair and crosses to the screen door and brings SISSER's wheelchair and SISSER out onto the porch.)

MOSES. You feeling better now, Sisser?

SISSER. Y'all having a party?

MOSES. Not a party exactly. Just a little get together. Sisser… I'd like you to meet my good friend Hank Hartley.

(HANK rises from his chair and extends his hand to SISSER in her wheelchair.)

HANK. It's a pleasure to meet you, Miss Bean…

(SISSER refuses to shake his hand.)

SISSER. You touch dead people with them hands?

MOSES. Sisser! Mind your manners!

HANK. That's alright, Moses. It's a fair question. *(To SISSER)* Why, yes…as a matter of fact…I do.

SISSER. Well, I ain't shaking your hand then.

MOSES. Sisser! That's not very nice.

HANK. I don't mind. In fact, I'm used to it. A lot of people are uncomfortable with my line of work. And I respect that. I don't take insult to it at all.

SISSER. *(To HANK)* What's it like working with dead people all the live-long day?

HANK. It's…sort of peaceful. And quiet. Real quiet. And… a little sad.

SISSER. *(After a pause; to HANK)* You want a Little Debbie?

(SISSER offers HANK an oatmeal creme pie she removes from the pocket of her housedress.)

HANK. *(Taking the snack cake from SISSER)* Why, thank you, Miss Bean. That's very kind of you.

(ANNABELLE returns from the house with more ice. She hands the tray to MOSES.)

ANNABELLE. *(To MOSES)* Sisser don't get no whiskey. She just gets tea.

(**ANNABELLE** *crosses to the flying cat. She covers the aquarium and returns it to its proper place inside the old cane house.*)

SISSER. *(To* **HANK***)* You got you a wife?

HANK. No, ma'am.

SISSER. So you ain't got you no kids?

HANK. No, I'm afraid that I don't.

SISSER. How come you ain't got no wife?

MOSES. Sisser…that ain't a polite question!

SISSER. *(To* **MOSES***)* You ain't got a wife, neither. (**SISSER** *looks at* **HANK**, *then* **MOSES***)* How come neither one of y'all's got a wife?

ANNABELLE. *(To* **SISSER***)* You just need to mind your own business, is what you need to do.

MOSES. *(To* **ANNABELLE***)* I was telling Hank you might be willing to take us out on the river for a quick ride in the boat before supper.

ANNABELLE. If y'all want.

HANK. *(Seeing the boat in the yard)* I don't think we're all going to fit in that little boat, Miss Annabelle.

(**MOSES** *and* **ANNABELLE** *begin to laugh.*)

ANNABELLE. We ain't taking that boat. I got me a motor boat down at the dock. We'll go in the big boat.

SISSER. I don't go out on the water myself. There's snakes and gators and lots worse things you can't see in that river.

(**ANNABELLE** *and* **HANK** *descend the steps of the porch.* **MOSES** *crosses to* **SISSER**.*)*

MOSES. We won't be gone long, Sisser. You gonna be alright here by yourself?

SISSER. When we gonna eat?

MOSES. As soon as we get back. The table is already set.

SISSER. Alright.

(**MOSES** *joins* **ANNABELLE** *and* **HANK** *down in the yard. The three of them vanish down the path to the* *river, leaving* **SISSER** *sitting all alone on the porch in her wheelchair.)*

(SISSER *begins to sing "What A Friend We Have In Jesus," then reaches over and pours herself a glass of whiskey, no ice, and takes a drink.)*

(After a few moments, **RUTH ANN MEEKS** *enters from the swamp. She is carrying a rifle and looking up at the sky, keeping watch for the flying cats.)*

(SISSER *stops singing and puts her drink down on the table.)*

(RUTH ANN *crosses to the steps of the porch, still holding the rifle.)*

RUTH ANN. I come to see Moses Bean.

SISSER. He just left.

RUTH ANN. Don't you lie to me, you fat bitch. I know as sure as I'm standing here that Moses Bean is inside that house trying to hide from me.

SISSER. What you got that gun for?

RUTH ANN. I went home and got Granddaddy Meeks' rifle just in case them flying cats come after me again. Let's see them wretched bastards come swoopin' down on me now.

*(***RUTH ANN** *raises the rifle and points it into the air.)*

SISSER. Why'd you kill Lurlene, the Palmetto Bug?

RUTH ANN. Palmetto bug?! *(Cocks the rifle)* I don't know nothing about no stupid palmetto bug.

(RUTH ANN *climbs the steps of the porch.)*

SISSER. What you doing?

RUTH ANN. I'm fixing to go inside that house and see Moses Bean, is what I'm fixing to do. I'm getting baptized tomorrow morning and I ain't got much time!

(RUTH ANN *makes a move towards the front screen door.)*

SISSER. *(Sternly)* Don't go in the house.

RUTH ANN. What, you gonna try and stop me? Why you can't even get your fat-ass up out of that wheelchair so how you gonna keep me from walking in that front door?

(**RUTH ANN** *opens the screen door and looks back at* **SISSER** *who is still sitting in the wheelchair.*)

RUTH ANN. *(cont'd)* Well? Ain't you gonna stop me? *(After a pause)* I didn't think so. *(Calling inside the house)* Moses Bean!

(**RUTH ANN** *enters the house. The screen door bangs shut behind her. Reaching over and holding onto the railing for support, Sisser slowly rises from the wheelchair. Singing "What a Friend We Have in Jesus,"* **SISSER** *slowly descends the steps of the porch and crosses to the wood pile. She reaches down and picks up the ax. We hear the strange sound that* **RUTH ANN** *heard earlier in the play as the windows and screen door of the house light up red again. The light pulsates, a deep blood red – an ancient heartbeat. The strange sound grows louder as* **SISSER** *approaches the house. Still singing,* **SISSER** *climbs the steps of the porch; the ax swinging back and forth at her side.* **SISSER** *puts the ax handle on her shoulder as she slowly opens the screen door and vanishes inside the house. The screen door slams shut behind her, almost like an exclamation point.*)

(*After a few moments, we hear a blood-curdling scream, then the sound of a loud gunshot coming from inside the Bean House.*)

(*Black out.*)

(**MUSIC:** *"Poor Ellen Smith" by Neko Case.*)

End of Act One

ACT TWO

Scene One

(MUSIC: "Outro With Bees" by Neko Case.)

*(A half-hour later. Lights rise to reveal **SISSER** sitting on the porch in her wheelchair. She is wearing **RUTH ANN**'s blue bow in her hair and has applied some of the girl's dark red lipstick to her mouth. **SISSER** looks grotesque, a sight to behold. She holds a miniature Bible in her hands.)*

(A dead body wrapped in an old rug lays halfway down the porch steps. We see two feet sticking out of the bottom of the rug. A few lose strands of hair can be seen sticking out of the top end of the rolled up carpet. Dark blood seeps through the rug, soaking the marshy ground.)

*(**MOSES**, **ANNABELLE** and **HANK** enter from the path that leads to the Watchalahoochee River. **MOSES** notices the rug on the steps and runs over to the porch.)*

MOSES. *(Horrified)* What have you done?! What in God's name have you done...?

SISSER. I didn't do nothing. I come out of the house and that gal that come here looking for you was laying dead in that rug down yonder-ways.

*(**MOSES** is shocked, not sure what to do.)*

MOSES. Annabelle... ?!

*(**ANNABELLE** crosses to the body. She bends down and pulls some of the carpet away, looks at the face and then quickly covers the body again.)*

MOSES. *(cont'd)* She dead?

ANNABELLE. She's dead alright.

MOSES. Oh, Jesus...Oh, Jesus Christ...! She'll go to prison... they'll give her the electric chair.

*(**HANK** crosses to the body as **ANNABELLE** climbs the steps of the porch and exits into the house.)*

HANK. Who is she?

MOSES. This crazy girl that had a crush on me. She was always coming down to the Texaco trying to get me to go out with her.

(**ANNABELLE** *returns from inside the house. She makes no mention of the rifle.*)

ANNABELLE. She did it in the front room. There's blood everywhere. On the walls...on the floor. She done killed that girl but good.

HANK. *(After a pause; very calmly)* You have to get rid of the body.

(**MOSES** *stares at* **HANK** *in disbelief.*)

MOSES. What did you say?

HANK. The body. You have to get rid of it.

ANNABELLE. He's right. And we gotta do it quick.

(**HANK** *crosses to* **MOSES** *and softly touches him on the shoulder.*)

HANK. Don't worry. It'll be alright. *(After a pause)* I'll help you.

(*There is a strange energy between the two men. Even* **ANNABELLE** *notices it.* **MOSES** *looks over at* **HANK**'s *hand on his shoulder, but doesn't pull away.*)

ANNABELLE. The Watchalahoochee. We'll take her out in the boat and throw her body in the river.

HANK. You'll have to put weights on it...otherwise she'll float.

MOSES. Oh, Jesus...*(After a pause; pulling himself together)* Okay...we've got some cement blocks on the side of the porch. We were gonna build a walkway through Buster swamp...a shortcut down to the River...but we never got around to it.

ANNABELLE. We'll need some chains...or rope...

HANK. *(To* **ANNABELLE***)* Something tells me this isn't your first time getting rid of a body.

(**ANNABELLE** *looks at* **HANK** *strangely.*)

ANNABELLE. There's rope in the cane house. *(Moving quickly)* Moses...help me...

(**ANNABELLE** *and* **MOSES** *cross to the cane house.*)

HANK. *(Making his way to the side of the porch)* I'll get the cement blocks...

(**SISSER** *starts singing again...*)

(**HANK** *crosses to the side of the porch and picks up a cement block. He then walks over and sets it down inside the small boat. As he returns to the side of the porch to get a second block, he steps on something. He looks down and picks up the hatchet, now covered in blood and hair. He holds the hatchet in his hand, then looks at* **SISSER**. *When she notices that* **HANK** *is staring at her, she stops singing.*)

HANK. *(cont'd) (After a pause)* Why'd you do it?

SISSER. *(After a pause)* I told her not to go in the house.

(**ANNABELLE** *and* **MOSES** *return from behind the cane house.* **ANNABELLE** *is carrying two mason jars while* **MOSES** *carries a thick roll of rope.*)

HANK. *(cont'd) (Holding the hatchet in the air)* I found the weapon.

(**ANNABELLE** *crosses to* **HANK** *and takes the hatchet from him.*)

ANNABELLE. You get the other cement block. We gotta get that gal out of here. Somebody's bound to come huntin' for her.

(**ANNABELLE** *places the hatchet inside the boat while* **HANK** *goes to retrieve one last cement block.*)

(**MOSES** *picks up the hatchet.*)

MOSES. Oh, Jesus God...

ANNABELLE. Moses.

MOSES. *(Almost in a trance; not quite hearing)* Ma'am...?

ANNABELLE. Put it down.

(**MOSES** *drops the hatchet inside the boat.*)

MOSES. It's the curse…it's the curse the old Sugar Witch put on us…we'll be found out…Sisser will go to the electric chair…we'll go to prison for helping her… for getting rid of the body. This is the end of it…This is the end of the Bean Family…just like the Sugar Witch's curse…(*Looking at* **ANNABELLE**) This is the way it's all supposed to end, ain't it? Ain't it?!

ANNABELLE. (*Ignoring* **MOSES**) Hank…I need you to help me tie up the body. Moses…give Hank some of that rope. Hank…I'll tie up one end…you tie up the other.

MOSES. (*Snapping back to reality*) What do I do?

ANNABELLE. Go in the house and get a box of salt and bring it back out here to me.

(**MOSES** *runs up the steps and enters the house, the screen door slams shut behind him, startling* **SISSER** *out of her trance. She begins to open another Star Crunch.*)

(**ANNABELLE** *and* **HANK** *tie both ends of the rolled up carpet tightly around* **RUTH ANN**'s *dead body.*)

(**MOSES** *returns from the house with a box of salt.*)

MOSES. Jesus Christ…the walls are covered in blood…

ANNABELLE. Forget about that now! We'll deal with that later.

MOSES. I got the salt. What do you want me to do with it?

ANNABELLE. Put it down on the porch for a minute. I need you to give me and Hank a hand here with this.

(**MOSES** *crosses to the body.*)

ANNABELLE. (*cont'd*) You two boys…y'all get both ends… I'll balance the middle…alright now…when I say lift… lift your end…on the count of three…one…two… three…lift!

(**HANK, MOSES & ANNABELLE** *lift the body and carry it to the boat.*)

(**SISSER** *begins to sing the old burial hymn,* "Shall We

Gather At The River.")

ANNABELLE. *(cont'd)* Alright now...lower it down in the boat. Careful!

MOSES. *(Getting sick to his stomach)* Oh, Jesus...Oh, Jesus God...

(They lower the body into the bottom of the small boat.)

ANNABELLE. *(To* **MOSES***)* You alright?

MOSES. I think I'm gonna be sick...

*(***MOSES** *runs behind the cane house and vomits.* **HANK** *begins to go to* **MOSES***, but* **ANNABELLE** *stops him.)*

ANNABELLE. Let him be. *(After a pause)* He'll be alright... he's just gotta get it out of his system. Moses is a pure soul. He ain't like us. He ain't used to darkness.

*(***SISSER** *stops singing.)*

SISSER. *(From her wheelchair on the porch; matter-of-factly)* Lurlene, the Palmetto Bug is dead.

ANNABELLE. *(Calling to* **SISSER** *on the porch)* That's the least of your worries.

*(***MOSES** *returns from behind the cane house, wiping his mouth with a handkerchief.)*

MOSES. *(After a pause; embarrassed)* I just got a little sick to my stomach, is all.

(Overcome with the urge to protect the younger man, **HANK** *puts his arms around* **MOSES** *and pulls him tightly to his chest.* **MOSES** *does not resist.)*

HANK. Don't you worry, Moses. Everything will be alright. Nothing bad's gonna happen to you. I'll see to that. *(To* **ANNABELLE***)* Now what?

ANNABELLE. Hank...I reckon you and me alone can handle getting the boat down to the river.

MOSES. What about me?

ANNABELLE. I got another job for you to do. But it's just as important. Probably more important if the truth be known.

MOSES. What?

ANNABELLE. Take that box of salt and go around the house…spread it on the ground in a circle…pour it heavy in the front…right here around the porch. Put extra salt in the doorways and on the window sills.

MOSES. Yes, ma'am.

HANK. *(To* **ANNABELLE***)* What will the salt do?

ANNABELLE. Keep the evil away. It won't stop it all…but it'll stop most of it from seeping into the house. I'll have to take care of what's already in there in a different fashion. *(To* **HANK***)* You ready, Hank?

HANK. Yes, Miss Annabelle. I'm ready.

ANNABELLE. Let's do it. Moses…you know what you're supposed to do now… .?

MOSES. Yes, ma'am.

ANNABELLE. I'll clean up the blood later. Get me some water…and bleach…and pour it all in a pail. Have it ready and waiting on me when I get back.

MOSES. Yes, ma'am.

ANNABELLE. You think you can handle all of that?

MOSES. Yes, ma'am. I can handle it.

(**MOSES** *crosses to the porch and grabs the salt container, then goes about pouring the salt around the porch and in the doorways and window sills.*)

(**HANK** *reaches down to grab one of the ropes tied to the boat,* **ANNABELLE** *stops him.*)

ANNABELLE. Wait. There's one thing I gotta do first.

(**ANNABELLE** *grabs the jars she brought over earlier from the cane house. She opens the lids, then hands* **HANK** *a long stick that's laying in the yard.*)

ANNABELLE. *(cont'd)* I want you to take this…go on over to the fire pit and shove one end of it down into the ashes…get it a little wet first so the ashes will stick…I burned that fire last night in honor of the ancients…so it's blessed and sanctified.

*(**HANK** takes the stick from **ANNABELLE** and does as instructed.)*

*(**MUSIC**: Underscoring #2.)*

*(While **HANK** is busy at the fire pit, **ANNABELLE** takes the thick sappy liquid from one of the jars and marks her forehead in three long horizontal lines. After a few moments, **HANK** returns from the fire pit and hands **ANNABELLE** the stick. **ANNABELLE** takes the stick and touches the body with it, making the sign of the cross down the full length of the rolled up carpet. She then takes holy water from the third jar and sprinkles it with her fingers over the body. She begins to hum a soft prayer. It is a strange, ancient tune; sacred and frightening all at the same time.)*

*(After finishing the strange prayer hymn, **ANNABELLE** breaks the stick in two over her knee and places it under both ends of rope atop the rug that is covering **RUTH ANN**'s lifeless body. **ANNABELLE** then places the palm of her hand over the carpet near the head of the body. Her touch is gentle, tender; a final blessing for the dead.)*

*(**MUSIC**: underscoring #2 ends.)*

ANNABELLE. *(cont'd) (To **RUTH ANN**'s body)* Poor, stupid girl. *(To **HANK**)* It's time.

*(**ANNABELLE** and **HANK** grab handles on both ends of the boat. They lift the boat and begin to carry it off into the swamp. They vanish on the path on their way to the river. The sun begins to set.)*

*(**SISSER** begins to sing "What A Friend We Have In Jesus" as **MOSES** climbs the porch steps. He starts to spread salt in front of the screen door.)*

SISSER. Where they going?

MOSES. To get rid of the body of the girl you killed.

SISSER. I wouldn't hurt a bug.

MOSES. It's a terrible thing for somebody to have to die in such an awful way. I wouldn't wish that on a dog.

SISSER. Are they gonna come and take me away?

MOSES. Why would anybody come and take you away if you ain't done nothing wrong?

(**SISSER** *is silent for a moment, then opens another Little Debbie Oatmeal Cream pie and begins to eat it.*)

SISSER. Did she say I done something wrong?

MOSES. Who?

SISSER. Annabelle.

MOSES. She don't have to say it. The proof's rolled up dead in the front room rug that's now on its way down to the Watchalahoochee River.

SISSER. Annabelle lies.

MOSES. You're the only I know that lies around here.

SISSER. Annabelle has secrets. Things you don't know about. *(After a pause)* But I know.

MOSES. *(Suddenly curious)* What do you mean by that?

SISSER. I know the secret. I got eyes to see…I got ears to hear. My ears heard a secret that ain't supposed to be told to nobody.

MOSES. What kind of secret?

SISSER. I promised Mama I'd never tell.

MOSES. You don't know nothing, so just shut up. You done caused enough trouble around here for one day.

SISSER. I can't tell you the secret…but you can ask Annabelle…see if she'll tell you. It's her secret. And it's all about you.

MOSES. If you say so. I ain't gonna stand here and argue with you.

(**MOSES** *pours the salt on the windowsill.*)

SISSER. *(Gazing off into the sky)* The sun's fixing to set. Gonna be a pretty night…

(*Suddenly* **SISSER** *begins to cry and wail, she screams and beats at her chest, tears at her own hair.*)

MOSES. *(Rushing to her side, trying to keep her from injuring herself)* What the hell is the matter with you?!

(SISSER *tries to tear the blue ribbon out of her hair.*)

SISSER. *(In hysterics)* Get it off me! Take it away! I don't want it no more! I don't wanna be buried with it! I don't wanna die this way! Don't let them bury me with it!

(MOSES *tries to remove the blue bow from his sister's hair as she fights him every step of the way.*)

MOSES. Alright! Alright! Stop fighting me! I'm trying to get it! Put your goddamn hands down and let me get it, will you?! Jesus God Almighty…you're out of your cotton-picking mind! Jesus, Sisser! Goddamnit! Put your damn hands down!

(SISSER *finally stops fighting* MOSES *and he removes the blue ribbon from her hair.*)

SISSER. *(Crying)* Is it gone?!

MOSES. *(Shoving the ribbon in the pocket of his jeans)* Jesus! It's gone! Now, just try and calm yourself down and quit all this carrying on. My nerves can't take no more of this. *(After a pause)* Jesus Christ, give me strength to endure!

(SISSER *begins to laugh.*)

And just what the hell are you laughing at?

(SISSER *suddenly stops laughing and beings to cry again. This time, however, it's a whinny, pitiful cry, not hysterical as before.*)

MOSES. What the hell are you crying for now?

SISSER. You don't love me no more…

(MOSES *bends down next to* SISSER*'s wheelchair, comforting her.*)

MOSES. Now, you just quit being silly. You know I love you. You mean more to me than anybody else in the whole entire world. *(After a pause)* So just quit your crying' 'cause you're acting like a big baby. You wanna go inside the house and wash your face?

(SISSER *nods "yes."*)

MOSES. *(cont'd)* You want me to take you in…or you wanna go in by yourself?

SISSER. You take me in…

MOSES. Alright.

> *(MOSES turns SISSER's wheelchair, opens the screen door and starts to roll her into the house.)*

SISSER. Moses?

MOSES. Yes, Sisser…?

SISSER. Can I get baptized one day?

MOSES. If you want to. It might be a little difficult with you being as big as you are and all…but I'm sure we can manage it somehow.

SISSER. I wanna get baptized in the Watchalahoochee. I wanna get all my sins washed away in the River. That way I can be like new. Will you help me to do that, Brother?

MOSES. I don't see why not. If that's what you want.

SISSER. That's what I want.

MOSES. Alright, Sisser.

SISSER. Soon?

MOSES. Soon.

SISSER. Promise?

MOSES. *(Softly)* Promise.

> *(MOSES kisses SISSER gently on the top of her head as the sun finally sets over the great Watchalahoochee River.)*
>
> *(Lights dim. End of Scene One.)*

Scene Two

*(**MUSIC:** "Make Your Bed The River Young Girl" by Neko Case.)*

*(An hour later. Lights rise to reveal nightfall at the Bean House in the middle of Buster Swamp. There is a small flame burning in the fire pit near the cane house. **ANNABELLE** is standing over the fire. She puts one end of her long stick into the flames and moves it in a circular motion.)*

*(**MOSES** and **HANK**, both holding flashlights, guard the house. They walk the periphery of the swamp, shinning their flashlights into the darkness, keeping watch.)*

*(**SISSER** is sitting on the porch in her wheelchair. She reaches into her pocket and pulls out the small miniature Bible from the pocket of her housecoat. The lipstick has been wiped from her mouth. She opens a large pocket book and removes a pair of pink panties, the panties that were inside **RUTH ANN**'s purse. **SISSER** takes the panties, puts them to her nose, smells them, then quickly hides them back inside the purse. She does this in secret. No one sees her.)*

The bottle of Jack Daniels is sitting on the top step of the porch.)

MOSES. *(cont'd) (To **ANNABELLE**)* Maybe nobody's gonna come looking for her. Maybe her Granddaddy didn't even like her. Maybe he's glad she's gone and out of his hair, too. Maybe Sisser did him a big favor by doing the terrible thing she done. Did you ever think of that? Huh? Did you, Annabelle? Did you?

ANNABELLE. Hush up, now! I'm taking care of business.

*(**ANNABELLE** stares intently into the flame inside the fire pit. Her mouth moves in a silent prayer as she petitions the Ancients.)*

I don't know if this is gonna be enough. The ancients is hard to stir. I may need more.

MOSES. More what?

ANNABELLE. More of what I need to undo what's been done.

*(On the porch, **SISSER** falls to sleep.)*

HANK. I think I see something off in the palmetto bushes.

*(**MOSES** crosses to **HANK** and shines his flashlight out into the darkness.)*

MOSES. What'd you see?

HANK. Never mind. It's just an armadillo. My eyes are starting to play tricks on me.

ANNABELLE. *(Gazing into the fire)* It was on this night...many years ago...

MOSES. The Great Flood.

ANNABELLE. The beginning of the curse. The night that turned the heart of the Sugar Witch to stone. This very night...many years ago...when the hurricane come out of the Gulf and changed everything forever. All the misery...all the pain...all the death...

HANK. *(Crossing to **ANNABELLE**)* I remember when I was a little boy...I overheard my grandfather...and my father talking about it.

*(**MOSES** crosses to the porch. He picks up the bottle of whiskey and opens it. He takes a drink, then joins **HANK** and **ANNABELLE** over by the fire pit.)*

ANNABELLE. All on account of one man's greed...one man's hatred...one man's prejudice...

HANK. They said the earth was so wet from the flood that the caskets in the graveyards came up from the ground. My grandfather said there wasn't enough coffins to bury the dead.

ANNABELLE. *(With great bitterness)* There were enough coffins to bury the white folks. Did your grandfather tell you that?

*(**HANK** looks away from **ANNABELLE**, ashamed of the truth.)*

(**ANNABELLE** *stares into the fire, almost as if she were in a trance, as if some haunted spirit were speaking its truth through her very being. We see the soul of the Sugar Witch long dead come alive once more.*)

(**MUSIC:** *Underscoring #3.*)

(*Above the porch in an old attic window [or just beyond the screen door], a horrifying* **APPARITION** *appears. Its face, like some hideous mask, stares out from the other side of the window or screen, twisted and terrible. Neither male nor female, the eyes glow a deep blood red. The "face" peers out from the house, watching the dark swamp. It is an apparition from Hell; the curse made manifest in demon form.*)

(**NOTE:** *The actor portraying Ruth Ann can be masked to appear as the apparition. If this is the case, the actor's face should NOT be seen by the audience.*)

ANNABELLE. *(cont'd) (Gazing into the fire, stirring the flame with her stick)* Terrible sight to behold…look if you dare. Bodies pile up…start to rot in the hot Florida sun. Vermin tear at the flesh…mad, hungry dogs carrying the carcasses of dead babies through the streets on the black side of town…East of the Great Watchalahoochee…nobody come to help…only the whites get help…the blacks are left to perish and rot…anger rising in the hearts of my people…rage now burning down deep in the soul of the Sugar Witch…curses falling from her dried, parched lips…curses you can't take back…curses you won't take back…

(**ANNABELLE** *comes out of her trance. She is herself again. The vision of the Sugar Witch vanishes from sight. The* **APPARITION** *is now gone.*)

(**MUSIC:** *underscoring #3 ends.*)

ANNABELLE. *(cont'd)* My own grandmother cursed this family…madness…sickness…death…every generation of the Bean Family would feel the burden of her pain…their pain…our pain.

HANK. Why would she curse the Bean Family? It doesn't make since. They didn't cause the hurricane. They weren't responsible for the flood.

(**MOSES** *sits next to* **HANK** *on the porch steps. He takes another drink of whiskey, then hands the bottle to* **HANK**. **HANK** *takes a swig from the bottle, then passes it back to his friend.*)

ANNABELLE. There was a dam built on the Watchalahoochee River by Moses' great grandfather…Buster Bean. Great Old Man Bean made the decision to open the dam so the black area on the other side of the river would get the worse of it…my people took the brunt of the flood waters. It was Buster Bean's decision…he saved his sugarcane fields…he saved his fortune…but in the end…he murdered hundreds of people…my people. Only a handful survived. My grandmother… the Sugar Witch…being one of them. She hated Great Old Man Bean for what he had done. So she cursed him and his blood. Anyone alive that carried the name Bean would suffer the Sugar Witch's curse. That was her vengeance. And so the Beans lost their fortune… they lost their place in the community…and slowly… over time…they lost their minds… they lost their lives…they lost their souls. All died young…all died in misery…damned for eternity.

HANK. Is there any way to break the curse?

ANNABELLE. Not any way I've ever been able to find. But the answer is out there…I can feel it in my bones…the answer will come…

HANK. How? How will it come?

ANNABELLE. It will come from the Ancients. We will end the curse tonight. Because if I don't…Sisser and Moses will feel the pain of the curse for the rest of their lives. Until the last Bean is dead…the curse will live on… like a rotten corpse that walks the night…haunting the world…screaming out at the moon for mercy… not allowed to rest…not allowed to die. (*After a pause;*

looking out into the swamp) The dead walk the swamp tonight.

(**ANNABELLE** *crosses to the edge of the swamp. We hear the distant, anguished cries of the restless dead.*)

ANNABELLE. *(cont'd)* Can't you hear them? Can't you feel them?

(Afraid, **MOSES** *moves closer to* **HANK**. *We hear the sound of the flying cats high above the swamp.)*

ANNABELLE. *(cont'd)* The cats feel it…there's no rest…not even for them. *(After a pause)* Come to me…the both of you…

(**MOSES** *and* **HANK** *cross to* **ANNABELLE** *as she moves back to the fire pit.*)

ANNABELLE. *(cont'd)* I know what I must do. The answer is in the old graveyard… .

MOSES. You won't be safe there.

ANNABELLE. I need dirt…from Mama's grave. We'll put a circle of protection around the house…but I can't do that until I take away the sin. The sin that's marked Sisser's soul…the evil deed she's done. It's got to be offered up to the ancients. Because…without their forgiveness…all is lost. For Sisser…*(To* **MOSES***)* for you… for all of us.

MOSES. I'll go with you.

ANNABELLE. No. I have to go alone.

MOSES. What if something bad happens to you…? You'll be out there in that awful graveyard all alone…

ANNABELLE. I promised your Mama…on her death bed… that I'd watch over you and Sisser. A promise to a dying woman can never be broken. *(After a pause)* Keep the fire going.

MOSES. Yes, ma'am.

(**MOSES** *tends the fire.*)

(**ANNABELLE** *crosses to the cane house. She returns*

carrying a large sack and a long stick.)

ANNABELLE. Keep Sisser in the house til I get back. Don't let her come down into the yard. The ground ain't been sanctified yet.

MOSES. She can't get down in the yard without help anyway.

ANNABELLE. Oh, is that what you think?

MOSES. You know Sisser can't do for herself.

ANNABELLE. Then tell me something, Moses Bean…if she's so helpless…how'd she get out of that wheelchair long enough to put a hatchet blade through that poor girl's skull? *(After a pause)* You think on that while I'm gone. Then maybe you'll realize everything ain't what it seems.

(MOSES is silent, not knowing what to say.)

(Back on the porch, SISSER awakens from her nap. She reaches for her box of bugs and opens it, peering inside.)

(ANNABELLE starts out for the graveyard. HANK stops her.)

HANK. Miss Annabelle…what do we do if they come searching for the girl?

ANNABELLE. Keep Sisser out of sight. *(After a pause)* And pray.

(ANNABELLE vanishes into the darkness of the swamp.)

SISSER. *(Calling to MOSES from the porch)* Where's Annabelle going?

(MOSES crosses to the porch.)

MOSES. To undo the terrible thing you done.

SISSER. *(Still holding the box of bugs)* The others are dead now, too.

(MOSES climbs the porch steps and takes the box from SISSER. He looks inside for a moment, then closes the lid.)

SISSER. *(cont'd)* Dead and gone.

MOSES. I'm sorry, Sisser. I know how much you loved 'em.
SISSER. Will you bury the rest with Lurlene in her spot?
MOSES. Hank…?
HANK. I'm here.

(**HANK** crosses to **MOSES**. **MOSES** hands him the box of bugs.)

MOSES. Grab the shovel over there and dig a hole in the yard. I need you to bury Sisser's palmetto bug collection.
SISSER. They're all dead.
HANK. What are you gonna do?
MOSES. I'm gonna take Sisser inside. She needs to rest a while.
HANK. I'll go ahead and bury the collection while you do that.
SISSER. (To **HANK**) Promise?
HANK. Promise.

(**HANK** goes down into the yard, takes the shovel and begins to dig.)

MOSES. (To **SISSER**) Here…let's get you inside…

(**MOSES** pushes **SISSER**'s wheelchair into the house.)

(As **HANK** finishes burying the collection, we hear the sound of the flying cats. **HANK** quickly covers the grave with dirt and backs up slowly to the house. He stares up into the night sky. The cats cast dark shadows across the moon high above Buster Swamp.)

HANK. (To the cats) Devils…all of you…monstrous Devils.

(After a few moments, **MOSES** returns from the house and crosses to **HANK** down at the edge of the cane field.)

MOSES. I left her in the front room. That way we can keep an eye on her. She'll fall asleep in her chair most likely…like she does most nights anyway.

(**HANK** offers the bottle of Jack Daniels to **MOSES**. **MOSES** takes the bottle and drinks from it.)

(The flying cats continue their screeching high above the

house.)

HANK. *(Looking up in the sky)* What kind of God creates such monsters?

MOSES. The same one that created us.

HANK. Maybe that's all we are. Human monsters. No different from those wicked things flying up there in the night sky.

MOSES. Not all of us are monsters.

HANK. *(Feeling the whiskey pretty good now; confessional)* I got into some trouble in Jacksonville, Moses. I did something bad. There was a…I had a…relationship…with someone who was…under-age. Fifteen. I was twenty-one. I spent some time in prison…I lost ten years of my life.

MOSES. But you're free now.

HANK. *(After a pause)* You don't think less of me?

MOSES. It's not for me to judge.

HANK. You have so much good inside you, Moses Bean.

MOSES. I'm no different from anybody else.

HANK. That's where you're wrong. You're like nobody else I've ever met. *(After a pause)* Why do you think I'm always bringing the hearse down to the Texaco?

MOSES. *(Innocently)* 'Cause you wanna keep it in tip-top shape?

HANK. Don't you know? *(After a pause)* I bring it in so I can see you.

MOSES. *(Not quite getting it; a little drunk at this point)* I enjoy seeing you, too, Hank.

HANK. *(Moving closer)* I'd do anything for you, Moses. I hope you know that.

MOSES. Even this terrible thing?

HANK. Even this.

*(**MUSIC:** "I Wish I Was The Moon Tonight" by Neko Case.)*

(There is a moment of silence between the two. **MOSES**

takes another drink from the bottle, then hands it to **HANK**. **HANK** *takes the bottle and finishes it in one long swig. He then looks at* **MOSES** *with an urgent longing in his eyes.)*

(HANK *tenderly brushes the hair from* **MOSES'** *forehead.* **MOSES** *glances over at the fire.)*

MOSES. *(Pulling away)* We can't let the fire go out.

(MOSES *crosses to the fire pit. He kneels down and stokes the fire with a stick.* **HANK** *finishes the bottle of whiskey, then sets the bottle down on the ground. He crosses to* **MOSES**, *kneels down, takes* **MOSES'** *face in his hand, and kisses him tenderly on the lips. After a moment,* **MOSES** *pulls away. He is both shocked and excited all at the same time.)*

MOSES. *(cont'd)* What are you doing?!

(MOSES *crosses downstage to the edge of the swamp.)*

HANK. *(Ashamed and embarrassed; following* **MOSES** *downstage)* I'm sorry...I thought you felt the same way that I –

(Suddenly **MOSES** *turns around and grabs hold of* **HANK***'s face with both hands. He presses his lips against his friend's mouth, passionately returning the embrace.)*

(HANK *begins to unbutton* **MOSES'** *shirt. As the two men continue to kiss,* **HANK** *removes* **MOSES'** *shirt.* **MOSES** *unbuttons* **HANK***'s shirt and begins to kiss him on his chest. Like the designer drug "ecstacy" – the love potion only intensifies the heat of the already existing attraction. The two fall to the ground, kissing and touching. They hold each other and begin to make love...)*

(From out of the swamp, there is the sound of a pick-up truck approaching the old house. **HANK** *and* **MOSES** *stop kissing and quickly reach for their clothes.)*

MOSES. *(In a panic)* Someone's coming! Hurry! Put your clothes back on!

HANK. Do you think it's them coming for the Meeks girl?!

MOSES. I don't know! I hope not!

(Headlights shine on the two men as the truck pulls up and parks beside the hearse off-stage.)

(GRANDDADDY MEEKS, *an elderly man in his 60's – 70's, enters from the swamp. The old man is drunk. He calls to them, slurring his words.)*

GRANDDADDY MEEKS. I come huntin' my grand baby. She ain't come home tonight. *(After a pause)* Y'all seen my little Ruth Ann?

MOSES. *(Blinded by the headlights)* No, sir.

GRANDDADDY MEEKS. She said she was going to the Bean House to see Moses Bean. *(To* **MOSES***)* Is that you? You Moses Bean?

MOSES. Yes, sir. I'm Moses Bean.

GRANDDADDY MEEKS. She wouldn't listen to me. I told her not to come out here to this godforsaken place.

MOSES. *(Not very convincing)* We ain't seen nobody named Ruth Ann.

GRANDDADDY MEEKS. *(Spits a wad of chewing tobacco on the ground)* Goddamn Beans...you think you're better than everybody, don't you? Always takin' things that don't belong to you...

MOSES. No, sir.

GRANDDADDY MEEKS. Always looking your noses down on the rest of us. I knew *(sarcastically)* Great Old Man Buster Bean. He kicked my dog in the head when I was a little boy just 'cause it got in his way. Buster Bean was a goddamn bastard. *(laughing)* And he died a mean, nasty death, too. Serves that son-of-a-bitch right.

MOSES. *(Offended)* That's my great-granddaddy you're talkin' about.

GRANDDADDY MEEKS. I hope you ain't as big a son-of-a-bitch as he was.

MOSES. *(After a pause)* We ain't seen your granddaughter.

*(***GRANDDADDY MEEKS*** takes a step closer to* **MOSES***.)*

GRANDDADDY MEEKS. I ain't going nowhere til I find my

baby. *(Calling into the house)* Ruth Ann?! Ruth Ann?! This is your Granddaddy calling you, girl! You come on out of that house and quit hiding from me, now! Come on home, now, darlin'. I ain't gonna whup you this time! I promise! Come on, now, Ruth Ann…it's getting late and I ain't had my supper! You come on home now and take care of your granddaddy!

HANK. He told you. Your granddaughter isn't here.

GRANDDADDY MEEKS. *(Stumbling; looking at* **HANK***)* I don't give a good goddamn what some Bean told me. You can't trust a goddamn Bean as far as the door.

MOSES. We haven't seen your granddaughter. You need to go on home now.

GRANDDADDY MEEKS. You Beans…y'all ain't nothing but a bunch of liars, cheats and fornicators. The whole damn lot of you. I warned Ruth Ann not to mix with your kind. But she got sassy with me…didn't want to listen to her granddaddy…*(Calling into the house)* Ruth Ann, girl! You get out here right this minute or I'll beat your ass, woman! Don't make me have to take off my belt…

*(***GRANDDADDY MEEKS** *starts to unbuckle his belt as he staggers forward.* **MOSES** *steps in front of him, blocking his path to the porch.)*

MOSES. Look, old man…I'll tell you one more time… *(raises his voice)* Ain't nobody inside that house that you know or got any business with.

GRANDDADDY MEEKS. Old man?! Who you calling "old man," you little piece of shit?! I may be old but I'll kick your ass till hell won't have it! I'm going in that house and getting my grand baby and if you know what's good for you…you'll get the hell out of my way…

*(***GRANDDADDY MEEKS** *takes a step closer to the porch.* **MOSES** *steps in front of him, blocking his way to the porch.)*

MOSES. Get back in your truck, old man.

GRANDDADDY MEEKS. Step out of my way…you little pansy…

(**MOSES** *raises his hands and pushes* **GRANDDADDY MEEKS** *back a step.* **GRANDDADDY MEEKS** *staggers, regains his balance, then takes a swing at* **MOSES***. The punch splits* **MOSES**' *lip and makes his head jerk back.* **MOSES** *falls to the ground as* **HANK** *rushes to his side.* **MOSES** *wipes the blood from his lip.* **HANK** *pushes* **GRANDDADDY MEEKS** *away from* **MOSES***.* **GRANDDADDY MEEKS** *almost loses his balance.* **HANK** *rushes back to* **MOSES**' *side.*)

HANK. *(Concerned and frightened)* Are you hurt?! Did he hurt you?!

(**GRANDDADDY MEEKS** *takes a few steps closer to the house as the screen door suddenly flies open to reveal* **SISSER** *standing in the doorway. She is holding the rifle that* **RUTH ANN** *brought with her to the house.* **GRANDDADDY** *takes one look at* **SISSER** *and starts to laugh.* **HANK** *grabs* **MOSES** *and pulls him out of the line of fire. The two stay off to the side of the porch, crouching down on the ground, taking cover.*)

GRANDDADDY MEEKS. Great day in the morning! Look at that fat-ass standing up there on that porch. I reckon you gonna try and stop me, too. Is that what you think? I bet you don't even know how to pull the trigger.

(**GRANDDADDY MEEKS** *places one foot on the bottom step of the porch. At that very moment,* **SISSER** *raises the rifle and fires a shot into the air.* **GRANDDADDY MEEKS** *lets out a "yelp" and backs up into the yard.*)

GRANDDADDY MEEKS. *(cont'd)* You crazy fat bitch! What are you trying to do…kill somebody?!

(**SISSER** *cocks the rifle and points it directly at* **GRANDDADDY MEEKS***. She fires the rifle somewhere in the vicinity of* **GRANDDADDY MEEKS**' *head. The bullet just misses him.*)

GRANDDADDY MEEKS. *(cont'd)* Jesus H. Christ! Don't shoot me! Don't shoot me! I'm going...! I'm going...! I'm backing up to my car now...don't get shaky, now... Don't shoot! I'm going on my way now... ..

(**GRANDDADDY MEEKS** *continues backing up, never taking his eyes off* **SISSER**. **SISSER**, *still standing on the porch, holds her position, rifle pointed straight at* **GRANDDADDY MEEKS**' *heart.*)

(*On the ground,* **MOSES** *and* **HANK** *watch* **SISSER** *holding the gun. Neither one moves an inch.*)

GRANDDADDY MEEKS. *(cont'd) (At the edge of the swamp)* Alright...you won this battle...but I'll be back. And I'll have the Sheriff with me. First thing in the morning... you'll have the law up your asses. We'll see how you like that. And I'll tell you one thing...if you bastards done anything with my little Ruth Ann...you'll have me and the law to answer to. There will be hell to pay! You hear what I'm telling you?!

(**SISSER** *cocks the rifle and fires one last shot into the air. At this,* **GRANDDADDY MEEKS** *runs to his car offstage. We hear the sound of the car quickly pulling out of the swamp, taking the headlights and* **GRANDDADDY MEEKS** *with it.*)

(*On the porch,* **SISSER** *stands frozen with the rifle in her hands while* **MOSES** *and* **HANK**, *still on the ground, look up at her in disbelief.*)

Lights dim. End of Scene Two.)

Scene Three

*(**MUSIC:** "Dirty Knife" by Neko Case.*

*(An hour later. Lights rise to reveal **MOSES** standing alone at the fire pit. His bottom lip is covered with dried blood from the punch he took from **GRANDDADDY MEEKS**. He stokes the flame, staring into the fire.)*

*(After a few moments, **MOSES** crosses to the porch. **HANK** has fallen asleep in the rocking chair. Careful not to wake his friend, **MOSES** enters the house through the screen door, then quickly returns with a blanket. He gently places it over **HANK**'s body to keep him warm. He then kisses **HANK** tenderly on the top of his head.)*

*(**MOSES** returns to the fire pit. He removes the blue ribbon he took from **SISSER**'s hair from his pocket and tosses it into the fire. He stands for a moment, watching it burn.)*

*(From out of the dark swamp, **ANNABELLE** enters. She is carrying her sack over her shoulder; the long stick clutched in her hand. Like Jesus returning from the Garden of Gethsemane, **ANNABELLE** appears defeated, resigned to the truth, knowing the terrible tragedy that has only now begun to unfold.)*

*(**ANNABELLE** watches **MOSES** for a moment from the edge of the sugarcane field. Staring into the fire, he does not see her right away. A look of love falls over her face, then the terrible sadness returns. Stooped over, back bent from carrying the enormous emotional and spiritual weight, the Sugar Witch approaches **MOSES** at the fire pit.)*

MOSES. *(Seeing her)* Annabelle!

*(**MOSES** rushes to help **ANNABELLE**. He puts her arm around his shoulder and leads her to a crate in the front yard.)*

ANNABELLE. *(Dropping her sack to the ground)* You kept the fire going.

MOSES. That's what you told me. I've done everything you asked of me. I placed the salt just the way you said…I went around the whole house.

ANNABELLE. Where's Sisser?

MOSES. In the house. Sleeping.

ANNABELLE. And Hank?

MOSES. On the porch. He fell asleep in the swing. I think he had a little too much to drink. I thought I'd let him rest a while, too.

ANNABELLE. What happened to your lip?

MOSES. Ruth Ann's granddaddy come looking for her. He punched me in the face when I wouldn't let him in the house.

(**MOSES** *crosses to the cane house and picks up the rifle that* **RUTH ANN** *brought to the house.*)

MOSES. *(cont'd)* Sisser scared him off with this...

(**MOSES** *hands the rifle to* **ANNABELLE**.)

MOSES. *(cont'd)* Ruth Ann must've brought it with her when she come back to the house that very last time. She must've had it with her when Sisser...*(he stops, unable to say the word)* Sisser must've hid it somewhere in the house.

(**ANNABELLE** *holds the rifle in her hands.*)

MOSES. *(cont'd)* He said he's coming back. He said he's coming back in the morning. And he's bringing the Sheriff with him.

ANNABELLE. We won't get away with this, Moses. It can't be undone. I thought I could help Sisser. But I can't do it.

MOSES. Didn't you get the dirt from your Mama's grave? I thought that's what you said...you said you could fix it if you went to the cemetery.

ANNABELLE. I never said I could fix it. I said I would try. Never said I could for sure.

MOSES. I don't understand...you said you were going to speak with the sugar witches...beg 'em for mercy...

ANNABELLE. The ancients spoke loud and clear. And I know what I gotta do. What we gotta do. *(Touching* **MOSES***)* It's a heavy burden, Moses. It'll haunt you and break you if you let it. *(After a pause)* Don't let it.

MOSES. You're scaring me.

ANNABELLE. I can only save you. No one else.

MOSES. But what about Sisser?

(**ANNABELLE** *shakes her head "no."*)

What'll they do to her when they find out the terrible thing she's done? What will become of her?

ANNABELLE. Electric chair, most likely. Or…if she' lucky… they'll lock her up in Eustis…where she'll sit and rot with the rest of the crazy, lost souls.

MOSES. *(Starting to cry)* I can't let that happen, Annabelle! *(After a pause)* I know! We'll run away! You and me… and Hank…we'll all run away together. We'll take Sisser far away from Sugar Bean…where no one will ever find her!

ANNABELLE. The curse will follow. Wherever you run… you'll have no peace.

MOSES. *(Pleading to* **ANNABELLE** *for some other way)* She needs me, Annabelle…! You know how much she needs me! She couldn't survive without me…she'd be so scared…

ANNABELLE. The dead have spoken…there's no other way. *(After a pause)* I can save you but you'll have to leave Sugar Bean and you'll have to leave it forever. And you can't never come back. Never.

MOSES. But what about you?

ANNABELLE. It's too late for me.

MOSES. I don't believe that.

ANNABELLE. Don't matter if you believe it or not. It's still true.

MOSES. So, what do I do? What's the answer, then?

ANNABELLE. Even a rabid dog…deserves some mercy… some peace.

(**ANNABELLE** *touches the rifle softly with her hand.*)

MOSES. *(Horrified)* What are you saying?!

ANNABELLE. Save her from a worse fate, Moses. If you love her…you'll do this…put her out of her misery. Put her down.

(**ANNABELLE** *holds the rifle out, wanting* **MOSES** *to take it. He moves away, recoiling from the gun.*)

MOSES. She's not some mangy old dog! *(Defiantly)* No! I won't do it! And you can't make me! There has to be some other way!

ANNABELLE. There is no other way. If you love her…you'll do this for her. This one last thing.

MOSES. *(An anguished cry)* No! I can't…

(**MOSES** *covers his face with his hands.*)

No!

(**MOSES'** *cries awaken* **HANK** *on the porch. He calls out to his friend.*)

HANK. Moses?! Are you alright?!

(**MOSES** *shakes his head "no"; tears streaming down his face.*)

ANNABELLE. *(Calling to the porch)* He needs you, Hank. Come to him…

(**HANK** *hurries down the porch steps. He goes to* **MOSES**, *puts his arm around him and comforts him.*)

MOSES. *(Sobbing; to* **HANK***)* I have to put her to sleep…I have to put Sisser to sleep…I can't let them take her…they won't understand…they'll hurt her…they'll hurt her bad…I have to put her somewhere safe…

HANK. She knows you love her, Moses…she knows that…somewhere in her sick mind…she knows it…

MOSES. *(Trying to convince himself)* It's the only way… .

(**MOSES** *buries his face in* **HANK***'s chest, sobbing.* **ANNABELLE** *watches, her face a mask of pain.* **HANK** *holds* **MOSES** *tightly in his arms.*)

HANK. I'll help you…you don't have to do it alone…

ANNABELLE. It'll be morning before long. That old man will be back soon. And he'll have the Sheriff with him.

There's no more time.

(**MOSES** *collects himself, pulling his grief inward. He understands what he must do. It will be done in love. He accepts what is to come. He will make it beautiful.*)

(**MOSES** *rises to his feet.* **ANNABELLE** *hands him the rifle.*)

ANNABELLE. *(cont'd) (Tears falling down her face)* Through the back of her head. She won't feel it. It'll be quick. She won't suffer.

(**MOSES** *refuses the rifle.*)

MOSES. No. Not like that. *(After a pause)* She wants to be baptized. We'll do it in the river. I promised her. I'll keep that promise. I'll baptize her myself. I'll lower her into the water... and then... when she needs air... I just won't let her back up. Her sins will be washed away... she'll be clean... she'll be free.

ANNABELLE. The white dress I made for her... the one with the pretty lace around the collar and the sleeves... she never wore it. It's clean. That's a nice dress, Moses.

MOSES. *(Wiping the tears from his face)* Yes, ma'am. It's real nice. *(After a pause)* I'll get her ready.

HANK. *(To* **MOSES***; gently)* I'll go in with you.

MOSES. No. I need to be alone with her. There's some things I need to say. Just her and me. No one else.

(**MOSES** *crosses to the porch. He climbs the steps and vanishes inside the house. The screen door shuts gently behind him.*)

(*Back in the yard,* **ANNABELLE** *hands the rifle to* **HANK**.)

ANNABELLE. Here.

ANNABELLE. *(cont'd)* In case he can't go through with it. *(After a pause)* Will you help him, Hank? If he can't go through with it...if he can't finish it when the time comes...will you help him do this terrible thing that's gotta be done?

HANK. *(Taking the rifle from* **ANNABELLE***)* Yes, ma'am.

ANNABELLE. And then when it's over…will you take him away from here?

HANK. Yes, ma'am. Far, far away.

ANNABELLE. Where you think you might be headed off to?

HANK. I don't know. California. Mexico maybe.

ANNABELLE. Make it someplace pretty. Someplace where he'll forget. Someplace where the ghosts can't find him.

HANK. Yes, ma'am.

ANNABELLE. *(After a pause)* Do you love him?

HANK. *(Tears in his eyes)* From the first moment I laid eyes on him.

ANNABELLE. Good. 'Cause he's gonna need you. You be good to him. He's my…*(she stops herself)*.

HANK. I'll take care of him. I promise.

ANNABELLE. You don't ever wanna find out what happens to a man who breaks his promise to a sugar witch.

HANK. *(Smiling)* Yes, ma'am.

ANNABELLE. *(Walking to the edge of the cane, peering out into the night)* I know too much. I've lived too long. *(After a pause)* But there's one story left to be told…before this night comes to a close. *(After a pause)* So sit down. And listen to every word. The day will come when you'll have to tell this story to the one you love.

(HANK sits down on the crate as ANNABELLE begins to tell him her final story.)

(MUSIC: Underscoring #4.)

ANNABELLE. *(cont'd) (After a pause)* I loved someone once. A long, long time ago. I was fourteen. We met by the Watchalahoochee River… it was summer and we'd go swimming together… just the two of us… laying there… on the banks of the river… the warm sun shinning on our backs. She was a child bride… her name was Emmeline. She was fifteen. We fell in love that summer. Every moment apart was pure misery. I ached for her like a baby aches for its Mama. Emmeline's daddy had forced her to marry the old man and by the time we met...she'd already given him a daughter. But she didn't love him. She loved me. And so she figured out a way for the two of us to be together.

(**ANNABELLE** *turns back to look at the house.*)

ANNABELLE. *(cont'd)* She talked the old man into bringing me on as help. Someone to cook and clean...and help her with the chores. In this very house... here on the edge of Buster Swamp.

(**ANNABELLE** *stares off in the direction of the river.*)

I knew about the curse on the Bean Family...I had heard the story ever since I was a little girl...on the Indian Island. My grandmother, the sugar witch had warned me...but I didn't care...the curse meant nothing to me. All that meant anything to me was Emmeline. *(After a pause)* When you're young...you're foolish... you don't know where the road might lead. You think you got all the time in the world to be young...to be free...to be in love. *(After a pause)* I got old man Bean to build me this cane house...*(points to the house)* He built it so I could do my work on the side. He didn't mind...as long as I gave him a cut of my earnings. *(After a pause)* At night...when he'd go off to bed...Emmeline would come to me...and we'd make love... out here in this cane house...just the two of us. We'd laugh and sing songs and whisper little secrets in each other's ear. We went on that way for twelve years...for twelve years... our secret was safe.

HANK. The old man never caught you?

(**ANNABELLE** *returns to the fire pit as she continues the story.*)

ANNABELLE. I made a special brew. And every night...when the old man would go to bed...Emmeline would slip some of it into his medicine. When he drank it, he'd fall into a deep sleep. Emmeline would sneak back in the house and climb into bed with him just before morning. *(After a pause)* We talked about running away together… but that never came to be.

*(**MUSIC:** underscoring #4 ends.)*

HANK. What happened?

ANNABELLE. This one night…Emmeline forgot to give him his medicine. He woke up in the middle of the night and seen she was missing. That's when he found us together…out here…in the cane house.

*(**ANNABELLE** crosses to the cane house.)*

He beat Emmeline. Beat her right here in the yard. Nearly killed her. And then when she was able to get herself up off the ground…he sent her to the house. Told her he'd deal with her later. I told her to do as he said…I didn't want him to beat on her no more. I weren't as strong then as I am now. Old Man Bean…he had the Devil in his eyes. I was scared of him. Scared of what he might do. Turns out…I had good reason to be.

HANK. What did he do, Miss Annabelle?

ANNABELLE. He took me in the cane house…and he beat me. He beat me worse than he beat Emmeline. And after he got done beating me…

*(**ANNABELLE** touches the wall of the cane house with the palm of her hand.)*

ANNABELLE. *(cont'd)* He raped me. Right on the other side of this wall. *(After a pause)* He did it to humiliate me. Said he was gonna teach me a lesson. Prove to me I weren't nothing but an ugly nigger. That's how he put it. *(After a pause)* Who was I to think I could have his wife? These was the words he was using all the while he was on top of me. *(After a pause)* But what he didn't know was that Emmeline had been standing here by the window…she had seen what he done to me. And she was waiting…hiding right here against this wall.

HANK. What did Emmeline do?

ANNABELLE. She had picked up the axe from the woodpile…right here. *(ANNABELLE points to the chopping block)* And when Old Man Bean come around the corner… she swung that axe and caught him right on top of his head. Split his skull right in two.

(ANNABELLE stomps her foot on the ground.)

ANNABELLE. *(cont'd)* His body fell to the ground. Old Man Bean was dead. Dead as could be. Right here…in this very spot.

HANK. God almighty…

ANNABELLE. I buried the body…out there…in the swamp. As far as the town folks knew…Mr. Bean had run off… leaving his young wife and thirteen year-old daughter to fend for themselves. *(After a pause)* You're the first living being I ever told this story to.

HANK. What happened then?

ANNABELLE. Not too long after…we learned that I was gonna have a baby. It was old man Bean's, of course. *(After a pause)* The baby had Mr. Bean's coloring, mostly…only a shade of mine. He looked white. White enough to pass. Emmeline come up with the story. She loved to read the Bible. The story of the baby Moses was her favorite. You see…she didn't want him to know that he was made in hate…in ugliness. *(After a pause)* And for a while…we were happy. We was a family. Me and Emmeline…and our little boy. Our precious little boy…

HANK. Moses…

ANNABELLE. That's right.

HANK. He's your son.

ANNABELLE. By that time…Sisser was already showing signs that she weren't quite right in the head. But we loved her anyway. We took care of her the best we could.… all the while hoping and praying it'd all turn out good in the end. *(After a pause)* But that weren't meant to be. The curse was as powerful as ever. Emmeline got sick. She held on as long as she could...but she just weren't strong enough. She was such a little thing. *(After a pause)* She died in the very same bed I give birth to Moses in. Right there...in that old house. In the room...at the back of the hall.

HANK. So in the end...the Sugar Witch...your grandmother...wound up cursing her own blood. *(After a pause)* All these years...how could you keep from telling him you were his mother?

ANNABELLE. I promised Emmeline on her deathbed that no matter what happened...I'd never tell Moses the truth. I promised her that I'd keep the secret. I'd protect him. I'd protect Moses from the truth. And I'd do whatever I could to protect them both from the Sugar Witch's curse.

HANK. Why have you told me this?

ANNABELLE. Moses needs to know the truth. But I can't be the one to tell him. I can't break my promise to Emmeline because that promise is all I have left of her.

HANK. I understand. You want me to tell Moses the truth about who he is.

ANNABELLE. One day...when he's strong enough to hear. Only then will he understand what's about to come. *(After a pause)* But promise me one thing, Hank Hartley...when you tell him...whenever that time comes... let him know he was loved by the sugar witch. Let him know that the woman he thought was his mother was a woman I loved more than life itself. Will you tell him that, Hank? Will you tell him that for me?

HANK. Yes, ma'am. I'll tell him.

ANNABELLE. *(After a pause; putting her hand on **HANK**'s shoulder)* Take care of my boy.

HANK. I will.

ANNABELLE. Now, I have to give you something... .

(**ANNABELLE** *crosses to the cane house and returns with a small metal canister.*)

ANNABELLE. *(cont'd)* Y'all gonna need all the money you can to get out of town and get far away from here. It's money I been saving from the sugar brew…my life's work. Give it to Moses for me.

(**ANNABELLE** *hands the canister to* **HANK**.)

HANK. Why can't you just give it to him yourself?

(**ANNABELLE** *is silent.* **HANK** *understands.*)

HANK. *(cont'd)* Thank you. Thank you, Miss Annabelle.

ANNABELLE. *(Looking off into the sugar cane field)* One last thing…tell Moses…somewhere in the sugarcane field is fine with me. Who knows…? Maybe I can bring it back to life again.

(*The screen door opens on the porch.*)

(**MUSIC:** *"Star of the Country Down" by Yo-Yo Ma [from "Appalachia Waltz"]*)

(**MOSES** *is holding* **SISSER** *by the arm, helping her walk.* **SISSER** *is dressed in her white gown that* **ANNABELLE** *made for her. She is using an old cane to help keep her balance. She wobbles a little with each step but* **MOSES** *has a firm hold on her. He guides her down the steps of the porch, helping her to keep her balance. Looking almost like a groom with his enormous bride, the two cross down-stage to* **ANNABELLE** *and* **HANK**.)

SISSER. *(To* **ANNABELLE***)* Brother's fixing to baptize me in the Watchalahoochee River. I'm going to Heaven now.

(**ANNABELLE** *can not even bring herself to speak.*)

SISSER. *(cont'd)* Thank you for making my pretty dress.

ANNABELLE. *(Fighting back tears)* You're welcome, Sisser.

MOSES. *(Softly, with great tenderness)* Sisser…are you ready?

SISSER. Is the water gonna be cold?

MOSES. No.

(**SISSER** *smiles*

MOSES *takes* **SISSER***'s arm and leads her down the path to the river.* **SISSER** *is unsteady on her feet, yet determined and proud.*

(**HANK** *follows* **SISSER** *and* **MOSES**. *He stays a few steps behind them, allowing* **MOSES** *to lead the way. He carries the rifle in one hand, the shovel in the other.* **HANK** *takes one last look at* **ANNABELLE** *– their eyes meet. It is good-bye.* **MOSES**, **HANK** *and* **SISSER** *vanish down the dark path through the swamp to the Watchalahoochee river.)*

(**ANNABELLE** *watches as the other three disappear into the night. She looks at the house, lightly touches the railing on the porch. She looks out into the swamp, towards the river. She seems at peace. She slowly crosses to the cane house – reaches out and almost touches the wood, then pulls back. She crosses to the fire and removes a small sack from her bag. She unties it and puts on a bracelet made of bones. It rattles as she slips it on her wrist. She then pulls out the purple bottle of poison. She removes the cork stopper, looks up in the sky, then drinks the poison from the bottle. She places the stopper back on and slips the bottle back inside her purse. She stares into the fire, turns away, and quickly runs her hand over the fire – the bracelet rattles. The fire immediately goes dark. For the first time, we actually witness the power she holds over the elements.* **ANNABELLE** *takes one last look into the sugar cane field and smiles.)*

(**ANNABELLE** *slowly ascends the porch steps and sits down in the rocking chair. She closes her eyes. After a moment, her head falls to the side. She is gone.)*

(Lights dim. End of Scene Three.)

Scene Four

*(**MUSIC:** "Things That Scare Me" by Neko Case.*

*(One hour later. At rise, we see **HANK** entering from the sugar cane field with a flashlight and shovel. He takes the shovel he is carrying and crosses to the cane house where he gently leans it against the wall.)*

*(On the porch are two large army bags filled with clothes and belongings. **HANK** crosses to the porch and picks up one of the bags and waits for **MOSES** in the yard.)*

*(The screen door opens and **MOSES** walks out onto the porch. He takes the blanket he covered **HANK** with on the porch and stuffs it into one of the army bags. He hands the bag to **HANK**, then walks back inside the house. **MOSES** picks up a red gasoline can. He splashes the gas on the walls and floors just inside the screen door. **MOSES** looks at **HANK** down in the yard, then removes a matchbox from his pocket. He lights the match and tosses it inside the house. He closes the screen door and descends the porch steps to the yard. When he reaches the edge of the sugar cane field, **MOSES** looks back at the house. We see smoke coming from the windows, then the flickering of orange flames inside the rooms of the old dark house.)*

*(The two men watch the house for a brief moment, then turn and walk away. Suddenly remembering something, **MOSES** rushes back to the cane house and disappears inside. He quickly appears from the old work shack carrying the flying cat aquarium in his arms. The cloth is still covering it. He joins **HANK** down in the yard. The two stand watching the flames engulf the house, their backs to the audience. As the lights begin to dim, we see the silhouette of the two men framed in the foreground of the burning house. **MOSES** kisses **HANK** as **HANK** puts his arm around **MOSES**' shoulder.)*

(The dying sugarcane field and swampland begin to turn an eerie shade of deep, dark orange. As we hear

the terrible sound of the flying cats echoing high above the ancient, haunted swamp world, **MOSES BEAN** *and* **HANK HARTLEY**, *hand-in-hand, vanish from Sugar Bean forever.)*

Lights dim.)

And the curtain falls.

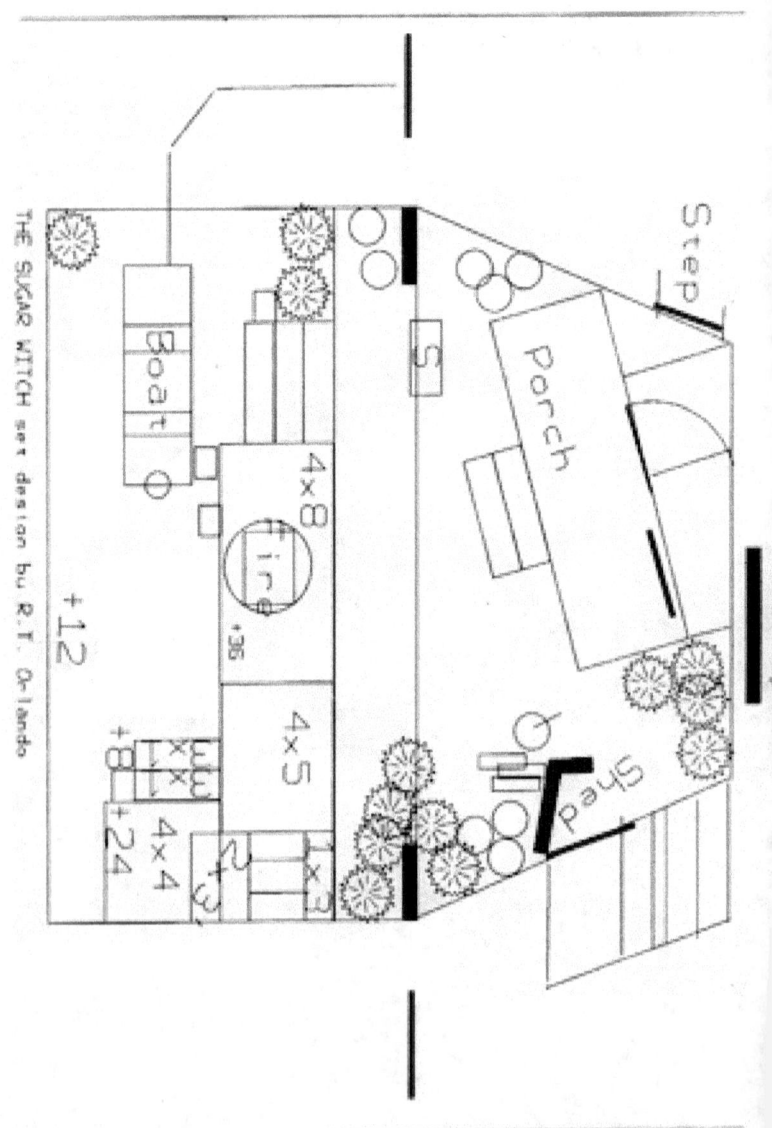

THE SUGAR WITCH set design by R.T. Orlando

From the Reviews of
THE SUGAR WITCH...

"Spellbinding...a gem of special effects, dead bodies, silent demons, flickering campfires and flying cats...eerie... chilling... moody...[*The Sugar Witch*] embraces gay/lesbian themes as heartily as anything you'll get south of San Francisco...[a] gender-reversed Sleeping Beauty!"
- *Metro Weekly* (Silicon Valley)

"A hauntingly creepy delight...lyrically written... a standout... quality play...intriguing... impressive...wonderful...(a) story of decay, violence and transformation...Li'l Abner meets William Faulkner... [*The Sugar Witch*] is filled with weird, surreal, stageworthy dramatic moments and situations...a satisfying balance between gothic horror and humor!"
- *Palo Alto Daily News*

"Sanders has a colorfully twisted imagination, a sharp-tongued way with one-liners and uniquely vulnerable characters who have no desire to live ordinary lives."
- *The San Francisco Bay Times*

"Bewitching!"
- *San Jose Mercury News*

OTHER TITLES AVAILABLE FROM SAMUEL FRENCH

DEAD CITY
Sheila Callaghan

Full Length / Comic Drama / 3m, 4f / Unit Set

It's June 16, 2004. Samantha Blossom, a chipper woman in her 40s, wakes up one June morning in her Upper East Side apartment to find her life being narrated over the airwaves of public radio. She discovers in the mail an envelope addressed to her husband from his lover, which spins her raw and untethered into an odyssey through the city... a day full of chance encounters, coincidences, a quick love affair, and a fixation on the mysterious Jewel Jupiter. Jewel, the young but damaged poet genius, eventually takes a shine to Samantha and brings her on a midnight tour of the meat-packing district which changes Samantha's life forever—or doesn't. This 90 minute comic drama is a modernized, gender-reversed, relocated, hyper-theatrical riff on the novel Ulysses, occurring exactly 100 years to the day after Joyce's jaunt through Dublin.

"Wonderful... Sheila Callaghan's pleasingly witty and theatrical new drama that is a love letter to New York masquerading as hate mail... [Callaghan] writes with a world-weary tone and has a poet's gift for economical description.
The entire dead city comes alive..."
- *New York Times*

"*Dead City*, Sheila Callaghan's riff on James Joyce's Ulysses is stylish, lyrical, fascinating, occasionally irritating, and eminently worthwhile... the kind of work that is thoroughly invigorating."
- *Backstage*

SAMUELFRENCH.COM

OTHER TITLES AVAILABLE FROM SAMUEL FRENCH

JACK GOES BOATING
Bob Glaudini

Full Length / Comedy / 2m, 2f / Interior

Four flawed but likeable lower-middle-class New Yorkers interact in a touching and warmhearted play about learning how to stay afloat in the deep water of day-to-day living. Laced with cooking classes, swimming lessons and a smorgasbord of illegal drugs, *Jack Goes Boating* is a story of date panic, marital meltdown, betrayal, and the prevailing grace of the human spirit.

"An immensely likable play [that] exudes a wry compassion."
- *The New York Times*

"Endearing romantic comedy about a married couple and the social-misfit friends they fix up. Witty and knowing and all heart."
- *Variety*

"Glides effortlessly from the shallow end of the emotional pool to the deep end."
- *Theatremania.com*

SAMUELFRENCH.COM

www.ingramcontent.com/pod-product-compliance
Lightning Source LLC
Chambersburg PA
CBHW070647300426
44111CB00013B/2311